THINK LIKE

A unique, practical guide to help you understand life from your horse's point of view

Michael Peace & Lesley Bayley

YOUR HORSE

David & Charles

A DAVID & CHARLES BOOK

First published in the UK in 2001

Copyright Text © Michael Peace and Lesley Bayley 2001
Copyright Photographs © Bob Atkins 2001

Michael Peace and Lesley Bayley have asserted their rights to
be identified as authors of this work in accordance with the
Copyright, Designs and Patents Act, 1988.

A catalogue record for this book is available
from the British Library.

ISBN 0 7153 1169 7

Printed in Italy by Milanostampa SpA
for David & Charles
Brunel House Newton Abbot Devon

Contents

Where It All Began

The more you work with horses the more you realise how much there is to know. I remember once talking to a man who had worked with horses all his life. He explained the problem to me very clearly by drawing a circle in the dust on the ground as a sort of pie chart, and told me to imagine this circle as being all there is to know about horses. Then he drew a segment in the circle of about 5 degrees, to show what *we actually know*. He drew another segment of about 20 degrees to represent what *we know we don't know*. He pointed to the remaining 335 degrees – this was what *we don't know we don't know*.

I didn't realise the significance of this at the time, but I now realise it really is incredible how little knowledge a person can get away with and still make a name for him or herself in the horse world. This is the nature of horses. Horses spend their lives filling in the gaps. The American trainer Ray Hunt says that even if you're only able to give 10 per cent you can guarantee that your horse will come up with the rest.

■ Everyday encounters that we take for granted may be a source of distress to a young horse, so use your imagination to think up different situations so that you build up his confidence in this new world

I started to work with horses at the age of 12 in a trotting racing stables at weekends and during my school holidays. I literally knew nothing about them; I couldn't even put on a headcollar. When I was 16 I went to the British Racing School at Newmarket. I wanted to be a jockey, and this was a good introduction to the racing world and what would be expected of me as an apprentice. Soon after I joined a proper racing yard and although the racing school was a good start, the real thing was quite different. It was a hard environment: whether you are a horse or a young apprentice jockey you are thrown in at the deep end and have to get on with it. It's a make-or-break approach. What I realised very early on was that, to a point, this 'get on with it', business-like approach was very important. It certainly developed me as a young rider, but I also learned that horses need this too. At times there were horses I didn't want to ride but I had to get on with it because it was my job. At times there were things some horses didn't wish to do too.

You have to go through a little bit of discomfort in order to develop and improve. Unfortunately in the horse world you see this approach go too far and become counter-productive. The job literally becomes more important than the horse or the person. This is obviously not a good situation, and is bad for morale. I realised very early on the requirement to balance the 'get on with it' approach with the needs of both horse and handler. When I'm working with a horse today it's very much a case of helping a horse through the difficulties to get the job done. There has to be a certain amount of effort made in order to achieve new things.

It wasn't too long before I got a reputation for riding the more difficult horses in the yard. Later I got the nickname 'Curer'. It wasn't that I was able to stay on them any better than other lads when they bucked, but more my ability to keep a horse happy enough so that he didn't feel the need to buck. I quickly moved on from riding the quiet ones to the more sensitive characters. Although it was uncomfortable for me at times it pushed me to develop my understanding of horses further and further, which I continue to do today. The more difficult a horse is the more there is to learn, and I really get a buzz when I get to work with the really tricky ones. I almost wish I could be challenged more.

My dreams of becoming a jockey were cut short because I began to grow too big and couldn't make the weight. Rather than stay as a lad in racing, I decided to do a three-year Thoroughbred Management Course in Witney in Oxfordshire. Here I learned a bit more about how the horse world was structured and how it worked as a business. I was still doing horses.

In the UK at that time there really wasn't a place for the work I was doing: it didn't stand alone in its own right. When I said that this was what I wanted to specialise in the college didn't really know how to accommodate it; they had lots of contacts in racing and other disciplines, but this was an unknown area. I decided to travel to America, Australia and parts of Europe to develop my understanding of the horse's nature, to meet and work with different horse breeds, and investigate different approaches to training. Occasionally I'd come across people who would have an interest in working with the difficult ones, as I did. In general there was a kind of bravado attached to these people; you had to be a bit tough and a bit crazy to want to do such a job. If I worked with these people it was more just to get the opportunity to work with difficult horses rather than learn their way of doing things. There was no toughness or bravado in my approach; I didn't want to battle with horses or wear them down. It was subtler than that; I wanted co-operation through respect, not force.

In principle my work is easy to understand. The difficulty and skill come in applying the principles to different horses and situations. What's most important to remember is that it starts with the philosophy and the methodology is attached to it. You can use any technique, method or equipment as long as you know how and when to use it – and never at the expense of the working relationship.

I think I was born with the understanding of the principles. I think it's natural to us all, but gets lost as we get older if we allow it. The ongoing

■ You only have one chance to make a good impression. For every new thing that your horse has to learn, you should set up each experience for maximum positive effect

development of my work lies in furthering my own awareness of the horse's nature and my own creativity to find a non-confrontational way through to a solution. Experience of different situations and application of the principles is ongoing.

I'll give you an example of what I mean. A lady came to see me with her horse, a four-year-old mare who had never really been successfully ridden. Ten seconds was the longest anyone had stayed on her. She'd always buck the rider off and had become very good at it. The owner was a bit snooty and had sent the horse to a professional trainer of young and problem competition horses to get her broken in. She'd injured riders and they'd tried to wear her down by lungeing her until she was tired, and even with a front leg tied up – she was capable of bucking people off on three legs. By the time I saw her she was really quite tough and exceptionally negative. She knew what she could do, and she meant to hurt people. She wasn't scared; she hated people.

When the owner dropped her off she was quite rude. She stormed straight past me into the barn and examined my stables, which was strange when you consider the horse had just come from a very smart yard that couldn't handle her at all. Anyway, luckily for the horse the owner decided my stables would do and she unloaded the horse and drove off. The horse was rude, impolite and aggressive and reminded me so much of the owner. I told my wife Susi that I was going to get the horse fixed and sent home in three days – just to make a point!

The next morning I tacked her up and began work with completely the wrong attitude. My motive was wrong. Normally my intention is to help a horse out, not to prove anything to anybody. I took her into the pen and jumped up so that I was leaning over her. In an instant she exploded and put me on the ground; she wasn't having anything to do with people and knew she didn't have to. That was unfair, I thought; she didn't even give me a chance. I went to her again. This time I leaned across her, swung my leg over and just as I was reaching for my right stirrup she shot off bucking and I was on the ground again. Okay, third time lucky, I thought. If I can just get my feet in the stirrups I'll be fine. I caught her, leaned across, swung a leg over, got my right foot in the stirrup and sat up. I said, 'Now you can do what you like!' – I'm in the saddle, with both feet in the stirrups, and it's going to take some horse to get rid of me.

One stride later I was on the ground again. To this day I don't know what she did – it was so quick, and such a big lesson for me. It reminded me why I had spent so many years developing my philosophy away from the bravado style of training I'd seen so often. I'm not particularly tough or brave, although many people think I am. The truth is that horses don't ever buck with me because I get the relationship right before I get on

■ Michael's approach is to work out a non-confrontational way of dealing with a horse's problems

them. This was just a lapse brought on by my emotional response to the owner's attitude towards me. I'd neglected to develop my relationship with the horse so that I could prove a point to the owner.

After the lapse on day one, I resumed my proven and tested approach to unridable horses. After three weeks the owner brought her groom to ride the horse, and the horse was sweet and happy to do anything for people. She rode willingly around the field, and is now taking part in competitions.

The owner was so polite when she came to collect the horse. Here was a horse who really didn't have to have a rider on if she didn't want to, and yet by getting the relationship right, she was able to make the decision to allow it. It was a very levelling experience. Any horse, any time, can put you on the ground if he wants to. They don't do it because they don't like trouble. Remember this next time you see somebody showing a horse who is boss!

Mutual respect is an essential ingredient to good horsemanship.

MICHAEL PEACE, *January 2001*

■ If a horse has never seen farm animals such as sheep and cows, ask a friendly farmer if you can move some around a field. Once a horse realises that they move away from him he'll find future encounters less daunting

Think Equus

Welcome to *Think Like Your Horse,* your unique and practical guide to making life easier for you and for your horse.

The ability to think like your horse will transform your life, and you will come across as someone who has that elusive 'natural' gift with horses. You know the kind of person: the one whose horses love to be with him or her, whose horses give 100 per cent, whatever the request. Such people have horses who perform any task without resistance, whether it's loading into a trailer, standing still while an injection is administered, jumping imposing cross-country fences, walking quietly past a huge, rattling combine harvester, negotiating a narrow, busy road, fording a fast-flowing river, and so on.

Owning such animals must result in a tremendous sense of pride, satisfaction and assured confidence, for when the partnership is strong there is a great deal of enjoyment for both horse and rider. Sadly, such a harmonious relationship eludes many owners. For these people horse owning often involves fear, frustration, tears, tantrums and confidence-sapping rides.

Their horses have numerous 'problems':

- Competing is no fun if your horse will not load.
- Riding out is not relaxing if your horse naps so badly that he refuses to leave his stable.
- An animal that attacks you when you enter his stable cannot be trusted.
- Working a horse in winter is tricky if the animal throws a complete wobbler as soon as he hears the clippers.
- Hacks are lonely affairs if you dare not risk company because your horse is uncontrollable when ridden with others.
- There is no pleasure in spending so much time trying to catch your horse that you barely have enough time to ride.

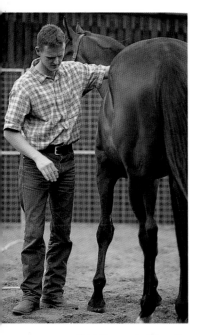

■ Think Equus principles will help you relate the horse's natural instincts to his behaviour in many different situations

Yet such occurrences are an all-too-common part of horses for many people. Why? In many cases people love their horses and have made considerable sacrifices in order to have them. They have 'done their best' to ride and care for their horses 'properly'. They spend money on lessons, gadgets, feed supplements, pressure halters and so on, yet within a short time of being 'fixed' their horse's particular problem raises its head again.

The reason their problems recur is because most people only have their difficulties papered over – they or their trainer do what they think is right. Unfortunately, because their solution is rooted in how the *human* views the problem, rather than how the *horse* views the problem, the difficulty still exists.

However, once a person has learnt to 'Think Equus' and applies the principles to all aspects of horsy life, 'problems' can be addressed and either solved or managed. In order to 'Think Equus' we humans have to make a quantum leap – for instead of acting and thinking like humans we have to curb our predator instincts and learn to view the world through the eyes of a prey animal, the horse.

Predator v prey

The fact that humans are predators and horses are prey animals affects everything we do with our horses. As an example, humans and horses think in entirely different ways. We have all seen the wildlife documentaries showing animals at the watering hole. Predator animals, such as the lion, think and act in the most direct way to achieve their goals – the lion can just march down to the water and drink whenever he is thirsty. However, prey animals such as zebra and antelope could not possibly adopt this approach – if they did they would die! Instead, they have to check out the situation, move slowly to the water, retreat if a predator appears, wait until it is safe; achieving their aim of drinking takes much more time and effort.

Translate this into a horsy situation. Imagine a horse that is difficult to catch. If you march into the field and walk straight over to the horse, it's likely that he will disappear into the distance. This is because the horse recognises the threat that you pose and reacts in the most natural way, by fleeing.

However, a different situation is created if you enter the field and wander around casually, initially making no attempt to go near the horse. The horse has no reason to see you as a threat and therefore no reason to run away. Gradually you can move into the horse's space, just as a new horse to the field may do. If you imitate equine body language and behaviour, advancing a little way towards the horse but moving away in an arc if he shows signs of being threatened by your presence, you will soon be able to approach, touch and catch him.

To achieve success, as in the latter scenario, you have to abandon your 'predator' instincts and adopt the thinking and behaviour of a prey animal.

Natural instincts

One of the keys to a successful relationship with your horse is for you to learn how to think more like him, and be imaginative enough to build his trust and confidence in you as rider or handler so that he has less need to act like a prey animal.

If you have ever started a young horse you will know that his natural instincts will be prevalent. Think of the horse living in the wild – if a mountain lion dropped on to his back death was highly likely. Imagine how the horse must have felt with that great weight on his back, with the lion digging in his claws and biting the horse's neck. Although none of this will have happened to our domestic horses their natural instincts are so well-programmed that they will know to react to this threat by bucking, rearing, plunging, twisting… anything to rid themselves of the danger. This is why young horses often react so violently when saddled for the first time.

■ Build your horse's confidence so that he happily accepts all aspects of modern life

Imagine how a young horse would feel if his first experience of being ridden also featured a rider who was scared and clung on with their legs and hands. You could not blame the youngster for thinking there was a dangerous object on his back that needed to be removed!

Life change

In their own ways, both the human and the horse have been successful, for both have survived. Along the way, though, life has changed dramatically for the horse: from the moment he was domesticated man has put incredible demands upon him. Horses have carried men into violent and bloody wars, they have worked on the land, drawing ploughs and harvesting crops, aided commerce by pulling canal boats, and have enabled men to conquer lands. Today they have many varied roles, from crowd control to competition, from ceremonial duties to being companions to thousands of leisure riders.

Some of these activities, for instance pulling gun carriages or being used to hold back riotous crowds, go against the horse's natural instincts. Any prey animal will flee from danger, so the sudden noise of guns delivering a salute would scatter most horses. However, army and police horses are testament to the fact that horses are very adaptable and can learn to cope with the many strange situations in which humans place them. So why aren't all horses as well behaved and well trained as, for example, police horses? The reasons are many: not all owners have the time to devote to such training; not all owners have the understanding to put the training into practice; or they may lack the necessary facilities for training. In addition, the horse may not respond well (not every police horse makes the grade) or there may be deep-rooted problems with a horse which his owner cannot resolve.

Some of these 'reasons' would be more correctly termed 'excuses'. An owner who takes on the responsibility of a horse has a duty to the horse and to themselves to make sure the animal is educated – otherwise they could be risking their necks every time they ride.

■ Horses are remarkably adaptable and willing to learn, providing you present every new experience in the correct way

■ Horses need time to work out what it is they should do

Solving problems

Many owners can only keep their horses if they work, which effectively means that their leisure time with the horse is limited. They may therefore be tempted to ignore a small problem with their horse. Instead of investing a little time and effort to address a small issue they leave it to fester until it eventually becomes much worse, and necessitates a great deal of time to sort out.

There are several keys to solving horse problems. One very important one is to think like a horse, and another is to act quickly before a little hiccup develops into a major disaster. How you use your time with your horse is also important; some people spend hours with their horses yet the animals are no better behaved or no closer to having their difficulties resolved. Effective time is what counts, not quantity of time.

In order to make effective use of time you need to be clear about what you are trying to achieve. You also need to recognise when the horse is taking steps towards the goal so that you can reward at the appropriate moment. However, you must also be committed to devoting whatever time it takes! It is a common fault for people to try and rush a horse.

When it comes to loading Michael has found that with many so-called difficult horses, it only takes seven minutes to complete the exercise. The horse just needs the time to assess the situation. However, human impatience often means that the handler becomes exasperated after three minutes and changes tactics, which is four minutes too early for the horse! As a result the handler has to spend much longer than seven minutes bullying or cajoling a horse into a trailer, perhaps even without ultimate success. If you take the attitude that you'll give the horse the time it takes to do the job, then the job gets done fairly quickly!

The rider or handler's attitude is, like time, another key to success. Horses are very sensitive to mood and atmosphere and will quickly pick up on the fact that you are scared, angry, upset or whatever. If you are anxious they too will be worried; most horses are natural followers and expect someone (such as you) to give them a lead.

Here are a few points that you should consider at this point in relation to your horse:

■ Horse owning is pretty time-consuming when all is going well. When you are experiencing difficulties there are even more demands placed upon you. If, to cap all this, you only just about tolerate your horse, you have to ask yourself whether you might be better finding another

■ Horses like to follow – but they must respect their leader

■ **Opposite:** Your partnership will benefit from time spent together just having fun – it's just as important to your relationship as the time spent in training

Take a few moments to think honestly about your current attitude towards your horse:
- **Do you love or just like your horse?**
- **Does your horse frighten you?**
- **If so, how much of the time you spend with him are you frightened or anxious?**
- **Why do you have a horse?**
- **How committed are you to working through any problems with your horse?**

equine partner. Humans and horses are all different and you may not be compatible with your current horse. There is no stigma attached to this – it is just a simple fact of life. If however you are devoted to your horse, getting through the tricky patches will still be hard but it will be more tolerable, simply because your attitude will be positive.

■ At some point in their lives most horse owners and riders experience fear. For some it is a fleeting moment which they deal with and then get on with their horsy activities. For others fear creeps in and insidiously grows until it controls every thought and action. If you recognise this scenario then you should seek help from an experienced instructor with a good knowledge of sports psychology, as conquering fear is often not feasible on your own. If, like many people, you experience moments of anxiety, be assured that this is natural and you can learn to control these. In addition, an understanding of the 'Think Equus' principles will give you more confidence in your own ability around horses.

■ Recognising and acknowledging the real reason for having a horse is useful for it may well affect your attitude to problem solving. As an example, if your horse was merely a status symbol, it is highly unlikely that you would be reading this book; you would probably not devote time to learning to think like a horse so that you could develop the necessary bond and partnership. On the other hand, if your primary motive for having a horse is to enjoy the relationship with another living being, you are probably open to anything which will move you closer to your goal. Your reasons for having a horse will also affect your commitment to working through any difficulties.

■ It is worth remembering that horses are also mirrors of their riders. If you are a stiff, unbalanced rider, your horse will be the same. He has no choice as he has to spend his day coping with you! There is another aspect to the mirror image – what you like or dislike about your horse often says a lot about what you like or dislike about yourself!

We hope we have set you thinking – not only about your horse but also about yourself and your motivations for having a horse. Over the next few chapters we'll be explaining the principles of 'Think Equus' and how you can use them in your everyday life with horses. The overall objective is to make life more pleasant for both you and your horse. Included in the chapters are some step-by-step guides to certain techniques – please ensure that you have mastered these before you try anything more complicated. Each chapter also has a checklist at the end so that you can confirm your understanding of the ideas presented. Please make use of these – they will help you to consolidate the principles and advice that we have given you. Good luck!

1 A NATURAL HORSE

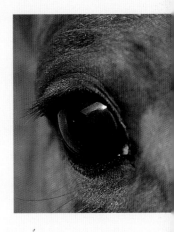

Above: A lovely kind eye. Most horses are genuine – it is our incorrect handling that can destroy this initial confidence and lead to problems such as aggression

Opposite: The unspoilt canvas – this is a critical stage in the handling of any foal and should not be wasted. He is at his most receptive at this young age, and it is vital to get things right now

If you really want to understand your child you have to step into his world and look through his eyes. This means throwing off your adult inhibitions and getting back in touch with your own childhood, when you were totally unaware of the worries and hassles now so common in your adult life.

As a child your interests were purely selfish – you could not understand your parents' requests or concerns as adults lived in a different world to you.

Trying to step back and think like a child isn't at all easy. Yet we were all children once! How much more difficult it is to put yourself into the skin and body of another animal. Yet that is what you must do if you really want to make a difference to your horse's life.

- **Living in a herd provides horses with two basic needs – survival and reproduction**
- **No matter how well trained your horse, there is a wild animal living inside him**
- **If you could step inside your horse's body, your view of the world would be completely different**

What is a natural horse? Is it a wild horse? Or the horse grazing in your paddock? Or are the two closely linked? Thousands of years may have passed since the horse was first domesticated, but we need to understand the past if we are to get the most from our horses today.

Many horse owners find the idea of horses being primarily working animals something with which it is hard to identify. The thought of horses living in the wild also seems extremely remote, especially in a country like Britain, which lacks the huge tracts of wilderness one associates with the USA or Australia where the mustangs and brumbies still run free. The fact that owners are removed from wild horses means that it is easy to forget that their leisure or competition horse, or companion horse, still has strong links with his evolutionary past.

How we keep our horses

As horse owners we may keep our animals in a variety of ways: at home if we have the land, in a rented field, at a livery or boarding barn, in a riding school or in a private yard. Our horses may live alone, or with any number of other equines. In some yards particular care is taken to keep compatible animals together; in other places little thought is given to the choice of field companions or stable neighbours.

If they are extremely lucky, the horses will have access to many acres of land, but in reality most have a very limited area in which to enjoy any freedom. Some unfortunate animals have very little time at liberty: for instance, some livery yards operate a no-turnout policy in winter, meaning that the horse spends 23 out of every 24 hours in a 12 x 12ft (3.6 x 3.6m) stable, the only release being an hour's ridden exercise per day.

From the human viewpoint, the horse is being provided with food, shelter, water, human friendship, the best veterinary care and so on. Surely the horse should be grateful? However, from the horse's point of view life is very different. So, how does the modern, domesticated horse see the world?

His way of life is a world away from that of wild or feral horses. It is important to remember that inside every domestic horse lurks a wild horse – the one with all his natural instincts who has evolved to live in a way far removed from the life so many horses now experience. In his current domesticated state he is denied access to equine friends, he is prevented from moving at will so his means of survival is threatened, and he is expected to surrender his feet to a 'predator' – us – which is a life or death issue!

It is an amazing testimony to the horse that the species can adapt so well and cope with the many demands humans impose.

It must not be forgotten, however, that just as some humans cope well with confinement and lack of company, there are others who do not, and horses are just the same. Some have adapted very well to domesticated life and seem relatively happy; some cannot cope at all and are often labelled 'problem' horses as they use any means at their disposal to handle the lifestyle imposed on them. Some horses tread the middle path, appearing to cope, but a closer inspection by a more 'horse-aware' individual would recognise the signs that the horse had 'closed down' and was not enjoying life to the full.

When we become aware of our horses' difficulties and implement a few simple changes, giving the horses a more natural lifestyle, the benefits are usually pretty immediate and positive. In order to do this, we first have to understand how horses would live if there were no human interference.

Life in the wild

The horse has evolved so that its natural order is to live in small herds, with one stallion, up to five mares and their young offspring. The herd moves over large areas, searching for food, safe from predators on account of their numbers and their ability to sense and flee from danger. If necessary, horses will also employ their defence mechanisms, by striking out, kicking, biting, rearing and bucking.

The unit of the herd facilitates two basic needs of horses: to survive and reproduce. Within an hour of being born the foals are on their feet as their very survival depends on their ability to move. Horses often sleep standing up (they have a unique locking mechanism in their legs so they can fall asleep and not fall over). At least one member of the herd will stay awake and be on guard.

■ Just being allowed the freedom to be a horse is appreciated!

HANDLING YOUR HORSE

- Horses appreciate quiet, consistent, confident handling. Remember this when you move around any horse.
- Think about how you touch your horse. If you slap him heartily he will not appreciate it, neither will he like a light, irritating touch. Try to observe a foal being licked by his dam: the touch is firm but loving. Keep this vision in mind when you touch your own horse.
- There is no place for noisy, aggressive behaviour around a horse.
- If you are stressed from work, or pushed for time, or upset about a home situation, do not try to teach your horse anything new. You will not be in the best frame of mind should any difficulties occur.
- If you are relatively new to horse owning then get into the habit of handling other people's horses as well as your own. You can learn something from each horse and this practice prevents you becoming blasé when in the company of horses.

While the adult horses in the herd often stay together for many years the young horses will leave at the appropriate time. The fillies will eventually become part of another stallion's herd, and the colts initially gather in bachelor groups before finding their own mares and forming their own herd. Although herds may temporarily join together, for example when at watering holes, they will usually keep their distance from each other.

As well as providing a place of safety, the herd structure allows for plenty of social interaction between members. Horses enjoy the company of their own kind and indulge in play throughout their lives. This play has the important function of teaching the young horses their social skills.

Much has been written about the organisation within the herd. There have been various ideas mooted, such as the stallion being perceived as the dominant horse, then the idea of the matriarchal mare, and of course there is the theory of the 'boss' horse and a resultant 'pecking order'.

■ Young horses are naturally inquisitive; this foal is more than happy to be fussed by Michael. The dam's easy acceptance of humans will affect her foal's view too

Different studies have examined the idea of a dominance hierarchy but we have to ask whether this is the most appropriate way of describing equine society. In the wild, the herd members appear to work together for the common good, with the role of leader being taken by more than one of the older horses. If you watch a group of domestic horses you will also see that one horse does not necessarily have ultimate power all the time. Horses seem to work in an atmosphere of co-operation which benefits everyone – something we will do well to remember when trying to train our horses.

When man interferes...

Domestic horses live in a false environment in that they usually have to share a much smaller land area than their wild or feral counterparts. In addition, instead of roaming over vast tracts of land, they return to the same field day after day, month after month. If the mix of horses in the field is wrong, there may well be more aggression than if the horses were able to get out of each other's way more easily.

Unfortunately for the domestic horse, man has also

■ Horses naturally seek the company of their own kind

imposed his ideas of the ideal community. Mares and geldings are often separated and stallions usually get the worse deal of all as they have to spend their lives without the company of their own species, except when they are required to perform their stud duties.

Livery yards often impose single-sex groups as they feel this is safer for their clients. This is because it is not unknown for several geldings to protect a mare from the attention of the mare owner! However, if a domestic herd is made up of a stable group of individuals then the sex of the members is not such a big issue. The key word here is stable: unfortunately, many horses in livery yards are put in fields where their companions change regularly, and so the herd is not given the chance to form a cohesive unit. In addition, the choice of companion can be arbitrary, with little attention given to existing friendships or whether a particular horse is a bully.

A little thought can make an amazing difference. We found this when Lesley was able to move from DIY livery yards to a private rented yard a few years ago. This meant that she could bring all her horses together for the first time. The herd includes a 21-year-old mare with her two sons, aged 5 and 3, a 27-year-old gelding who is the old mare's pair bond (a really good friend with whom she spends a great deal of time, in close proximity), another mare aged 13 and two more geldings, aged 24 and 18.

Since they have been together on a permanent basis the horses have been much more relaxed, happier and playful. When the youngest horse was weaned he stayed with the herd while his dam went to another yard. Many horses find weaning a very traumatic experience, but as this youngster's weaning was left until he was eight months old and he had the rest of the herd to look after him, he was very laid back about the whole procedure. Other members of the herd were seen to chaperone the youngster and one day, when an incident on the adjoining road alarmed the older horses, they all encircled him and took him off to a safe distance.

Lesley has noticed that although horses do play throughout their adult lives, her own horses have indulged to a much greater degree since living in their own herd. All the horses join in, with the older ones admonishing the youngsters if they become too boisterous. It has been interesting to see how the youngsters have been educated, by the other horses, as to the acceptability of their conduct. While the foals were at foot, their dam reprimanded them for misdemeanours. As these foals have grown up in the herd all the members of the group have contributed to their education and life skills.

■ Grooming is a pleasant and mutually beneficial process for horses, even though the sight of teeth being vigorously used may be off-putting for the human observer!

Not fighting, just ➡ playing

A common misconception is that horses are fighting each other when they are actually just playing. To humans, equine play can look a pretty rough-and-tumble affair, but it is important to recognise the difference between normal horseplay and aggressive or bully-like behaviour. When playing, horses may well show their teeth or their heels, but they do not usually cause serious harm to each other; if a horse is aggressive he has more purpose to his actions, and it is clear that he intends his kick or bite to hit home.

4

1 The foreleg strike is often seen, and doesn't have to be a sign of anger; these two play together every day and are good friends

2 Horses move each other around by 'biting' heads and bottoms, often without making contact. The ears are held flat back just as a precaution, to keep them out of harm's way

3 Normal behaviour in a group of horses: they will pull at each other's tails, snap at hindquarters, and so on – all part of the learning process

4 Play also takes place at great speed; they will swerve and kick out, but without making contact. Remember that happy horses play; unhappy horses do not

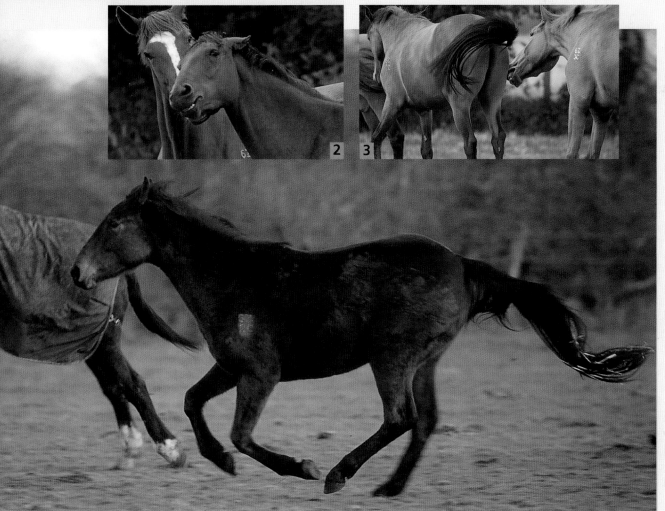

If you watch the interactions that occur within a herd it is easy to see why problems arise if horses are denied this kind of social living or if the mix of animals is out of balance. Some horses are unfortunately kept on their own, so their outlet for normal, healthy, horse behaviour is non-existent. This 'deficiency' has to show itself somewhere along the line and such a horse may well find himself labelled as a problem animal through no fault of his own.

Some owners protest that they keep their animals solo because of bad experiences in the past. Anyone who has owned a horse who was bullied by another will understand this feeling, but it is wrong to deny a horse the company of his own kind. Negotiations with livery yard owners can usually solve the problem, perhaps by removing the bullied horse and his constant companion to a separate field, away from the bully.

Problems with such horses are not just confined to the field. If an aggressive horse is stabled next to or close to his 'victim' and the horses can see each other then the 'victim' will still feel intimidated. The idea of horses having emotions is a difficult concept for some people to grasp, but many behaviourists and trainers have had to deal with horses whose problems are rooted in fear, either of people or other horses. There is also plenty of anecdotal evidence from ordinary horse owners of their animals showing emotions such as fear, jealousy, grief and affection.

GREETING YOUR HORSE

- Ask your horse's permission before entering his personal space. As you approach him, in the stable or in the field, quietly offer the back of your hand. This action is a non-threatening gesture and will be seen as such by him.
- Do not approach your horse head on. He has a blind spot directly in front of him. Always approach from the side so that he can see you coming.

■ Horses who are comfortable in each other's company, like these half-brothers, spend a lot of time together, grazing, playing and dozing in the sun

■ Once a horse has put distance between himself and something strange he will often stop and check out the situation

In addition, horses have what is known as their flight distance, that is the distance they put between themselves and something which frightens them. If danger is perceived horses usually run, and then stop and turn after a quarter of a mile or so, checking out whether the 'monster' is a real threat or not. The herd as a whole will also have spatial awareness in relation to other herds.

If you are aware of the horse's personal space then you can treat the horse with the respect he would expect, rather than simply intruding on his space in an aggressive way (which is how the horse will view it if you simply barge into his stable and so on). If you understand a horse's flight distance then you will realise why, when frightened, horses turn and run. The fact that you can prevent some horses from even running at all is a tribute to how that particular horse views you: as a leader and friend, and someone with whom the horse can feel safe.

Recognising personal boundaries

Conflicts of horse personality will also occur in the wild, but the resulting difficulties will not be so far-reaching because the two horses can simply avoid each other. However, when space is limited, this simple strategy for an easier life is not always available.

The space which horses keep between themselves and others varies according to each individual. We must never forget that every horse is different and may change from one day to the next. Humans have good and bad days – why shouldn't horses? Their lives and feelings are complex too.

Humans have their own personal space and do not like unwelcome guests invading it. The horse also has his own boundaries, allowing his pair bond to come really close, grazing or lying alongside him, maybe even eating from the same pile of hay or bucket of food. However, these privileges would not be extended to other horses within the herd with whom he is not so friendly. Horses recognise each other's boundaries and are aware that if they go uninvited into another horse's personal space they may be kicked out, literally! Young horses seem to blunder into other horses' personal space but their submissive mouthing (opening and shutting of the mouth, showing their teeth and tongue) lets the other horse know that they are not aggressive and are still learning the rules.

How does the horse perceive the world?

Always remember that the basic difference between humans and horses is that we are predators and they are prey animals. This colours everything we do. As predators we are used to getting what we want and our whole approach is very much goal-orientated. If we want to eat or drink we just get on and do so. If we want to get from A to B we just walk along the road, paying little attention to the roadworks, or the woman with the umbrella, or the washing blowing on a line in someone's garden. These things are not important to us.

However, the horse will not regard that walk along the road as such a simple task. Despite his thousands of years of domestication the instinct to survive is strong, so he will be worried by the hole in the ground, the large moving object and the things which flap into his vision, disappear and then just as quickly reappear. He has no way of knowing that these things are not life-threatening. All his senses are saying 'watch out, there could be danger here'.

Through careful handling and education we can prepare a horse to meet all kinds of 'hazards', and countless horses have shown that they can adapt, proving to be rock-solid riding horses. However, even the most bombproof animal can suddenly be spooked by an unexpected event – and when this happens he is just being ruled by his natural instincts for a split second. No matter how well trained your horse, there is always a wild horse living inside him, which is why he is alert and easily startled.

In addition to these strong natural instincts we also need to consider that he has a different vision of the world. Horses have very large eyes positioned high up to either side of their heads so that even when grazing they still have a good view of their surroundings. When you appreciate that the siting of the eyes ensures the horse has virtually 360-degree vision, and that by turning his head slightly he can achieve all-round vision, you realise that Mother Nature has given him a pretty neat survival aid! A horse moves his head from side to side while grazing, always ensuring he has a good view of what is happening around him.

The horse's highly mobile ears are another of his security aids. This, coupled with the large size and the funnel shape, enables the horse to accurately pinpoint where a sound is coming from.

Smell is another important sense, not only for recognising danger in the environment, such as fire or the presence of a predator, but also for acknowledging friends. One horse owner could not understand why her normally friendly horse suddenly backed off as she approached. Then she realised that there was one crucial difference – for the first time she was wearing a rather strong perfume! It took a few minutes of soothing talk before her horse could be persuaded to approach her again.

It is not uncommon for riders to recount tales of how their horses have suddenly refused to walk forward when riding over moorland. Some will even admit that they forced their horses forwards, only to find themselves in a boggy mess. In the wild horses test the ground if they are at all unsure – they will paw at the ground or stamp on it with one foot. Once satisfied that the going is safe they move on. We still see this behaviour now, and not just

HOW A HORSE'S NATURE SHOWS THROUGH

On a day-to-day basis there are many occasions when a horse's strong survival instincts affect his behaviour. This can lead to 'problems' for horse owners in the following ways:

- Your horse is a herd animal and may not want to leave his companions in the field. The uneducated rider/handler sees this as stubbornness.
- A horse is worried by dark, confined spaces – how is he to know that they are safe? He may therefore be difficult to load into a trailer or be apprehensive about going into stables. Often this is misinterpreted as wilful misbehaviour.

- A horse may lack confidence and so, out on hacks, gets upset and pulls if his equine companion is too far in front. His rider just feels that her mount is hard to control and so may resort to putting a stronger bit in his mouth.
- A horse backs off from a rider who enters the stable carrying a whip and then runs around so that the rider cannot catch him. Is the horse being naughty or is the memory of a beating in his stable, handed out by a previous owner, haunting him?
- A horse picks up his foot but starts to lose his balance. He tries to put his foot down but the handler refuses to let go and shouts at him as she thinks he is being difficult.

These are just a few examples. No doubt we can all think of incidents when we reacted in a way which, with the benefit of hindsight, we now recognise as being inappropriate. The horse does everything for valid reasons. The benefit of the 'Think Equus' philosophy is that you will understand the reasons and respond in a different way to your horse's predicament.

when riding across moorland or through water. Young horses being loaded for the first time will investigate the ramp, often with their teeth and feet, before stepping on it. Older, nervous horses may do the same. In either case, you should allow the horse to satisfy himself that there is no danger.

If you could step inside a horse's body for a short while your view of the world would be completely different. You would see and hear so much more, you'd be much more aware of your vulnerability and would be ready to run for your life if danger threatened. If, on top of all this, you had to face the world alone, you'd be much more nervous. Imagine how much worse you'd feel if a human then tried to make you do things, without communicating with you clearly and without taking your feelings into account.

Your horse need not feel so anxious – for by learning to Think Equus you can reassure him, communicate in his language and build a partnership where you will both benefit.

CHECKLIST Before moving on to the next stage of learning how to Think Equus, take a moment to reassess what you have read so far.

- It is important to remember our horse's evolutionary past because it has a tremendous effect on the way he behaves today, and provides us with guidelines as to how we can keep him happy and healthy in a domestic situation
- In the wild, the typical composition of the herd is one stallion with around five mares and their offspring
- A herd provides a long-term haven for its members, giving them safety from danger, the opportunity to find a mate, and friendship
- Horses play to learn and practise life skills, and for enjoyment
- The term 'pair bond' implies that two horses are really good friends and spend time in each other's company, grazing and eating in very close proximity
- The term 'flight distance' is the initial distance a horse runs to when he flees from danger
- Horses have virtually 360-degree vision
- A horse uses smell, touch and hearing to detect danger
- Although the horse has been domesticated for a long time his survival instincts are very strong and affect his behaviour
- Horses really thrive when they live in a small, stable group where careful consideration has been given to each horse's friendships

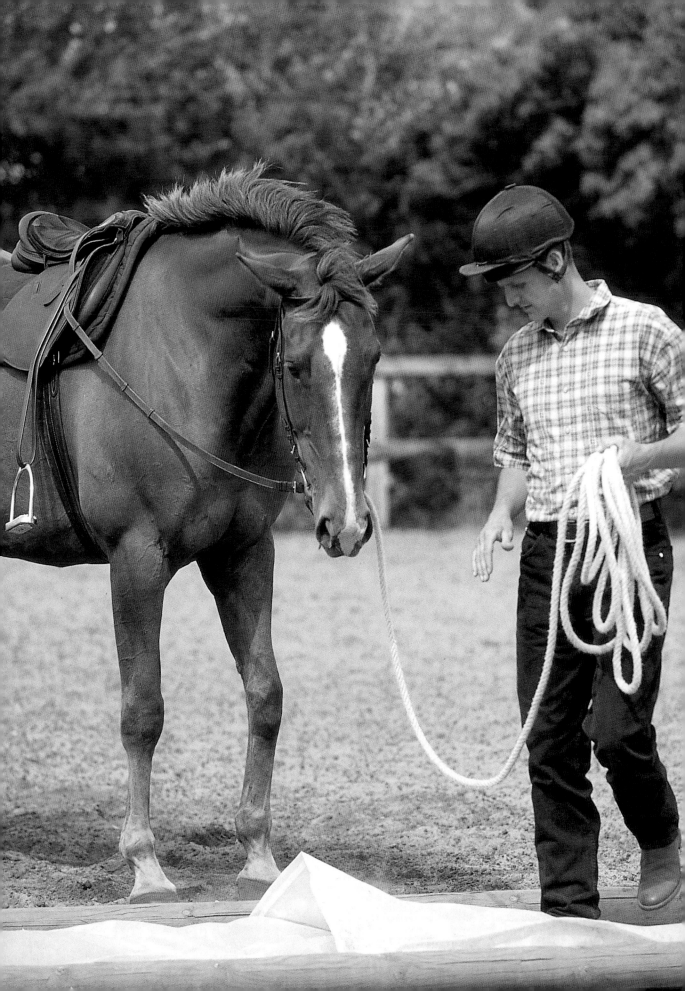

2 CROSSING THE DIVIDE

Imagine you're on holiday in a country where you do not know the language and where the locals do not speak your language. Just getting hold of simple things like food and drink, or somewhere to stay, can be difficult. If the locals then get angry at your efforts to communicate, or ignore you completely, life gets even worse.

Yet this is just what happens to horses. They use their behaviour, body language, and sound – everything at their disposal – to tell us how they are feeling; yet many riders, owners and handlers ignore the messages.

Above: Napping – that is, being reluctant to go forward – is quite a common problem and ruins hacking for many riders. In order to deal with the situation, the rider first has to determine the reason for the behaviour. If a horse is genuinely frightened of something, the last thing he needs is a tough attitude from the rider

Opposite: To overcome problems such as napping, you will need to get your horse to overcome his fears, whatever they may be. Having gained confidence from Michael's work with him on the ground, this horse will now be happy to be ridden over the plastic

- Pitch the lesson at the level and pace that suit the horse
- Give the horse the time he needs
- Do not presume anything
- Work second by second

Some people even start to put human interpretations on their horse's activities, for example 'the horse stopped at the first fence to show me up'! This may sound crazy, but if you listen to competitors at any local show you will hear countless wonderful excuses for poor performance in the ring. There may have been many valid reasons for the horse stopping at the first fence – insufficient training, lack of impulsion, conflicting signals from the rider, discomfort from jumping on hard ground – but certainly not the human emotion of revenge! Horses are horses and have a different way of thinking and behaving to humans.

We can learn to think like a horse and can understand how to train horses so that the horse too learns to stop and think when a problem arises rather than just running away. Transporting yourself into the horse's world and seeing situations through his eyes sounds simple; yet although people can often apply this principle to one scenario, they fail to do so with other situations. It can also be difficult to overcome a lifetime of thinking about things in a particular way. As an example, many riders have had drilled into them the idea that if a horse refuses to go past something when out hacking he must be *made* to go past and this must be done from the saddle. Getting off is seen as a 'defeat' as the horse has 'won'.

This is a common situation. Take the horse which spots the roadworks in the distance and lets his rider know by adopting the 'startle' position with his body (so alerting other horses to potential danger). If the rider is insensitive or inexperienced and cannot recognise this behaviour she may simply see that the horse is reluctant to move forward. She may therefore smack the horse and urge him on, using her legs, hands, whip and voice. As the horse is genuinely concerned about the roadworks the rider's actions are merely confirming his fears; his rider, who is supposed to be his leader, is acting in a strange and anxious way too.

If the rider continues with this activity she will soon have a battle on her hands because she is certainly not convincing her horse that he should move forwards – in fact, she is doing just the opposite!

However, if the rider adopts a more flexible way of thinking she can overcome the problem. Ideally she would have recognised the horse's genuine anxiety rather than misinterpret it. She now has the situation where the horse will not go forward. She can decide to just turn back and not go past the roadworks – and

if she has really wound her horse up this may be the only safe option. If so she needs to learn from the experience and ensure she does not repeat this 'no win' situation.

Something which she could have done right at the beginning of the incident was to get off and lead her horse past. The horse would not have seen this as a 'defeat' because he was not involved in any battle. On the contrary, he was anxious about the roadworks and wanted reassurance and help. By getting off, the rider is saying to the horse, 'It's okay, I'm the leader and it's safe for you to follow me'.

This is just the same as another horse providing a lead past a scary object, into the water jump, and so on.

SHIFTING YOUR THINKING

Making the switch from thinking like a human (predator) to thinking like a horse (prey) is not something that happens overnight. It is a skill you have to constantly work towards.

Whenever you come across a problem with your horse ask yourself these questions:

- Am I being fair in my request? Has my horse received sufficient preparation for this task – is he mentally, physically and emotionally ready?
- Have I been clear in my request? Does my horse understand exactly what is required of him?
- If I looked through my horse's eyes would my request be reasonable or not?
- Am I requesting or demanding?
- Have I caused my horse to lose confidence in himself or in me?

If more people did this, and answered honestly, they would see that their 'problem' horse is more likely confused, ill-prepared, worried, panicky; in fact, anything other than bolshy or difficult.

But, we hear you cry, there are horses who do just mess around for the hell of it and need to be told off. That's true, but are you 100 per cent sure you can tell the difference each time? If so, who is to blame? Is it the horse's fault or the fault of the rider/handler who failed to stop cheekiness turning into a problem?

■ This is typical body language, when one horse is telling another to get out of the way

Just as the horse would find comfort and courage from following another horse, so he would have followed his rider. Instead of setting herself up for a battle with her horse this rider could easily have won some brownie points from him – all it required was a shift of thinking.

Communicating with each other

If you want a horse that you can enjoy riding and caring for, you need to understand the equine communication system and how you can use this yourself. Horses communicate with each other using all their senses and their body language. They can understand the subtlest of signals – we are all probably telling our horses far more about our state of mind than we realise!

Use of the body   When a horse is relaxed his whole posture and body says so. His muscles are soft, his head may be lowered, and he may be resting a hindleg, his ears floppy, his lips relaxed, and his eye soft. There is no way this horse is going anywhere in a hurry.

However, if the horse is suddenly startled, his posture changes instantly. His entire body is prepared for flight: his limbs are immediately underneath him so he is ready to power off into gallop, his head and tail

carriage are high, his ears are pricked, the eyes are alert, he may show tension in his mouth and he will probably be snorting. Suddenly this horse looks bigger and has presence. This change is brought about for two reasons: so that the horse can flee, and so that he can also warn others in his herd of the possible danger.

These are the two extremes, the relaxed and the startle position. Yet the horse's body also gives away other information: tension, stress, illness, fear, anxiety and excitement can be communicated through his body appearance and movement. To interpret the signals properly requires knowledge of how the horse uses specific body movements and his senses.

The head and neck   If you watch horses in a herd you may see one approach another with his head and neck lowered and outstretched, possibly 'snaking', that is moving it from side to side. This signal is taken by other horses as a sign of aggression and is interpreted as 'get out of my way' or 'move on'. This type of aggressive behaviour would normally occur if the horse's earlier warnings of eye contact and ears back had been ignored.

Thrusting the head towards another horse (or human) is also a signal to be wary of. There is a distinct difference between a horse who is being menacing and one being inquisitive. Many horses will investigate your pockets for treats but their facial expressions, their ears

37

Do your homework first ➡

If a horse is frightened, hitting him or forcing him to go past a tractor or cross a stream, for example, only adds to his fear and teaches him that his rider or handler is not to be trusted! If you force a horse to do something when he is frightened, the potential for trouble in the future is increased. After any such incident the thinking rider will know that extra homework is required to ensure that he is better able to cope with unexpected situations. These photographs show how to accustom a young horse to coping with crossing something she initially finds worrying.

1 In the absence of a headcollar you can attach your line as shown here. This prevents the bit from being pulled through the horse's mouth as you work

2 Asking a young horse to work over a piece of plastic is a good character-building exercise. It teaches a horse to deal with a problem that she'd normally avoid. Here she's saying 'Do you really want me to do this?'

3 She realises that this is something that needs dealing with, so she takes a good look and, after a few seconds, takes one tentative step closer

4 The next step is not so easy, and the best she can do is to take a step to the side. It is important to recognise that she's still trying, and to tell her that the sideways step is good enough, so Michael gives her a rub on the head. A step backwards may indicate a lack of effort, or evasion, or it may just be too much for her. Sideways steps indicate a good effort and must be rewarded

5 Now she's really working at it, so Michael steps back across the plastic and opens up the space in front of her to get the job done

6 It's a bit scary, but she knows it needs doing and makes a decision to go for it… and receives a lot of praise

continued

5

6

7 The second attempt should be easier, but she needs just a few seconds to make the decision

8 Decision made!

9 Now she has to do it on her own. She'd like to say that it's too difficult…

10 …but she's going to give it a try

11 Michael feeds her plenty of slack rope as she makes the decision, and gives her plenty of praise again

12 It's important to consolidate the exercise by asking her to do it two or three times more – now she finds it really easy

Above: This horse is interested in what is going on in the distance, but he is not in full startle position as his hindquarters are too far out behind him

Opposite: All horses enjoy mutual grooming; it can look quite tough at times

Some horses cope with pressure by switching off so that they have a rather glazed look to their eye, as if 'the lights are on but no one's home'. We know of a mare that was badly beaten up by a so-called trainer. By the time the horse was returned to her owner there were no other physical signs to indicate what had happened. However, the owner immediately noticed the glazed look in the horse's eyes and eventually discovered the truth. It took two years of sympathetic rehabilitation before the horse was back to her old self and her eye was big, kind and soft again.

and eyes will be 'soft' and kind. When assessing a horse's intentions you must always take into account the whole picture rather than just one element.

Horses do have a wide range of facial expressions: angry, jealous, distressed, and afraid. Horse watching is great fun, very educational and a fantastic way to de-stress yourself – so take any opportunity you can to watch horses just being horses.

Ears   A horse's ears may face forwards, backwards or sideways to varying degrees. For instance, when a horse is alarmed by something in the distance his ears will 'ping' into forward position, as far as they can go. With certain breeds, such as Arabs, the inwardly curving tips to the ears add to the visual impression that the ears are in radar mode.

Attention may be focused in more than one direction at any time, so one ear pointing forwards and one backwards means that the horse has his attention split. This is often seen when horses are being ridden.

Ears that are flopping to the side mean that the horse is very relaxed – if you see this in a ridden horse it is a good sign. Take note of how the rest of the horse looks, as this will be a good indication of the level of – or lack of – tension in ridden horses.

Many people think that a horse that has his ears flat back is showing aggression. This may well be the case, but it is not the only reason. In the wild horses that are genuinely fighting (for example two stallions, or a horse trying to see off a predator) will lay their ears flat back in order to reduce the risk of injury.

Eyes   There is a saying that the eyes are the mirrors to the soul, and the horse's eyes tell the observant owner a great deal about the animal's state of mind. Take the time to watch a variety of horses being ridden and look at their eyes. If a horse is being pressured by a rider he may well have a worried look, and often the white of the eye will be visible. This also happens if a horse is angry, but there is a difference between anger and fear when reflected in the horse's eye.

Forelegs   When horses meet new field mates they often strike out with their forelegs; mares and stallions that are being introduced to each other do the same, as do horses at play. Equine games also include horses standing on their hindlegs and 'boxing' with their front legs.

If you watch foals you will see them investigating new things by pawing or stamping with their forelegs and feet.

Hindquarters A kick from a hindleg, or the double-barrel effect of both hindlegs directing a kick, is an extremely effective weapon for a horse. However, it is not normally used unless the horse's other warnings have been ignored. So if you know someone who has been kicked by a horse, you can guarantee that the person misread the situation and did not heed earlier warnings (given by facial expressions, position of the ears, a vocal message, presentation of the hindquarters and so on).

It is not unusual to see horses swinging their hindquarters round into the path of another horse – when the horses are playing this usually indicates that someone has gone too far. The offending horse is being told that unless he behaves a kick will be delivered. Watch a herd of horses playing and you will see this and the preliminary warning signs which, if

ignored, build up to this final warning. Unfortunately some horses also learn that presenting their backside in the stable can intimidate some humans!

Foals often swing their quarters round so that an obliging human can scratch them – this is fine when they are small, but a 17.2hh heavyweight doing this can be an awesome sight. The message is, therefore, to be careful what you allow a youngster to do!

Sense of touch As well as using their forelegs and feet to test for danger, horses also use their muzzles and very mobile lips to check out strange objects. Think how much a young horse uses his mouth to investigate everything from your coat and hair to his saddle and rugs. Be aware that this is normal behaviour for a young animal – so think about what you leave within his reach.

Touching also provides the horse with a means of reassuring himself and others. Mares will lick their newborn foals all over their bodies to clean them, but

Voice   A huge percentage of the communication that occurs among horses is related to body language and visual signals. With their skill at reading each other it is hardly surprising that they can transpose their skills to the human arena and read our body language well!

However, they do also 'talk' to each other using a wide range of sounds. The soft, low whicker is used to call to a friend, either equine or human. If you ever get the chance to observe a mare and foal within the first few days of the foal's life listen carefully to the mare's gentle calls. They are very different to those given to other horses: it is vital that mare and foal learn to recognise each other by sound as well as by smell, sight and touch.

When horses snort this usually signifies the possibility of danger; squealing generally indicates excitement or indignation (for example, perhaps, a mare who is not quite ready to accept a stallion's advances).

The fascinating aspect of equine communication is that horses all over the world can 'talk' to each other and be instantly understood. There are no language barriers.

this also helps to develop the bond between dam and foal. Horses that have strong bonds with their humans often make physical contact with their owners if they are at all worried.

Mares will teach their foals how to move by touching them, for example on the neck or hindquarters, to direct the youngster's movements. Touching can also be used by a mare as a reprimand, such as a shove with the nose if the youngster is too boisterous when suckling, or a nip on the backside if the foal does not move when told.

When horses groom each other a lot of rhythmical touching goes on. This has the practical value of ridding each other of parasites, can be soothing and also helps the relationship between the horses. Owners are advised to spend time grooming their horses to help the horse's health, but also because grooming 'gentles' a horse and improves the bond between horse and handler.

Sense of smell and taste   In the wild a horse would need to take note of the observations he made via smell and taste in order to survive. Domesticated horses still live by these rules – smelling dung so they know who has been in their field or stable, sniffing mares who are in season, carefully sniffing and snuffling in feed which has been laced with medicines, smelling the air and so on.

> ## WHAT DOES MY HORSE MEAN?
> - Friendly call – whicker
> - Danger call – snort
> - Excited call – squeal

Acting like a horse

Now that you have an idea of how horses communicate and can read the signs a little more, take a fresh look at your own horse. Is he happy? How can you tell? Are you looking at happiness from his point of view, or from your interpretation of horsy happiness?

Remember that a horse needs security and the comfort and company of his own kind. He needs to act like a horse. All animals have their own codes of behaviour for their particular species and we should not try to interfere with these or impose our values on our horses. Horseplay can look pretty intimidating to humans but it's a vital part of equine life. A horse that

plays a lot is happy and relaxed. It is always worth reviewing how you keep your horse – maybe he could have more time at grass, or different companions, or more challenges in his training programme. If you make any changes, observe your horse and compare his activities to his previous lifestyle to ascertain whether he is enjoying his new life more.

By looking through your horse's eyes you will understand that, for instance, napping and bolting are natural behaviours for a horse that lacks confidence or is frightened. The key to overcoming the problem is to widen the horse's comfort zone in his training so that his confidence increases and he can tolerate various

Above: Whatever you do with your horse, keep a close eye on his body language – he will let you know if he is unhappy for any reason. This horse is clearly uncomfortable about being rugged up

Opposite: Horseplay takes all forms; this five-year-old horse is grabbing hold of his dam at the base of the neck, something which stallions do during mating

situations. To achieve this you need to think like a horse. You can also stack the odds in the trainer's favour, for example, when starting a young horse why not keep the horse in the most natural conditions – living out in his well-established herd. The process of being educated is enough for him to think about without the added complication of being confined to a stable and kept away from friends.

The same applies when introducing new horses to a herd. Do not just put all the horses together but take the time needed to integrate the new horse carefully. This will mean putting the new horse in a field alongside a middle-ranking horse from the herd. Once the two are talking and grooming over the

REMEMBER...

There is always a reason for a horse's behaviour, and the more you can see life from the horse's point of view the easier it will become to pinpoint the real source of any problem.

fence without any hassle they can be put together. The combination is then allowed to increase their bond before being exposed to other members of the herd.

Just like people, individual horses have their own stress thresholds. Most horsy people will have seen horses which weave, windsuck, crib-bite, box walk and so on… all so-called vices. Just using the word 'vice' implies that the fault for the problem lies with the horse, when quite the reverse is true. Many 'vices' arise because of inadequate management. As an example, horses have evolved to eat for at least 16 hours out of every day. If a horse is confined to a stable and his hay runs out after an hour he has a lot of time to fill. He has a psychological need to chew – in chewing hay a 550kg horse will make 3,500–4,500 chews to eat 1kg of hay, compared to around 1,200 chews for 1kg of concentrate feed. Therefore if a horse is denied or has restricted access to hay or grass, the time he would normally spend eating will be reduced – hence doors are chewed or grasped and the horse draws in air. His owner may see him and fit a collar or some other device to discourage the habit. This only increases the stress for the horse, as he now has no way of alleviating his natural instincts.

Using your body language to best advantage

Being more aware of the messages your horse is sending you is one half of the equation. The other half, which is very important, relates to the messages you are transmitting, consciously or unconsciously. We already know that horses can read our body language and are attuned to our emotions – the question is how do we ensure that the messages they receive are the ones we intended to send?

Body language can be used in various ways. The aggressive stance requires the person to keep their head up and maintain eye contact with the horse, make their physical appearance bigger by holding their arms out to the sides and keep their shoulders high and square. If you look at the photographs of Michael working you will not see such an extreme position. By contrast, the passive stance necessitates bowing of the head, keeping shoulders rounded and low, arms at the side, and avoiding eye contact with the horse.

If you experiment and adopt the aggressive and

Using the right body language

You may have read or heard about adopting body language to show that you are in either an aggressive or passive frame of mind. Although Michael uses his body to convey messages to horses he does so in a more subtle way, adopting an assertive rather than aggressive stance. The horses have no problem in understanding his signals. Many of the horses he deals with are already troubled by their contact with humans and appreciate Michael's less offensive tactics.

1–3 Michael is demonstrating passive body language here: note the lack of eye contact and his rounded shoulders. It is clear that there is no sign of aggression or assertiveness in his posture and behaviour

4–5 Even when sending the horse round, Michael's body language is assertive rather than aggressive; he is still relaxed and easy, and so inspires confidence in the horse. In the second photograph he is thinking ahead and planning where he should position himself in order to make it easy for the horse to change direction

passive stances with your horse they do work. However, if you do as we advise and fine-tune the aggressive stance so that it becomes subtler, you will soon discover that not only does it work but also that it is like whispering to the horse, rather than shouting.

The power of your intent

As well as learning to use your body to your advantage you need to gain control over your mind and emotions. If an incident with your horse has worried you it can be hard to master your anxiety and face up to a problem. It is crucial to deal with issues when they are small and manageable rather than let them mushroom into huge dilemmas. Work carefully through Chapter 3, First Principles, and follow the step-by-step guides. Be reassured that once a horse owner has gained respect and attention from their horse, and mastered leading, that other areas are not so daunting. Many of the horses we come across have their difficulties rooted in the fact that the horse does not have sufficient respect for his handler on the ground. Once this respect is established other 'problems', such as being difficult to load or clip, become easier to solve.

DON'T RUSH THINGS

Having confidence in the techniques you use and in your own ability is essential. Through the pages of this book you will see the techniques working, and you can also attend Think Equus courses and demonstrations to gain further insight. Strengthen your belief in yourself by being realistic about what you can safely tackle and by breaking tasks down into sensible chunks.

Use this book, use your head and do not try to walk before you can run. Give yourself, and your horse, the time it takes to achieve the goal.

■ Your body language, and the way you use your body, are equally important when in the saddle: you have to be clear in your intentions, ie in this case to help the horse make the decision to walk over the plastic

CHECKLIST Before moving on to the next stage of learning how to Think Equus, take a moment to reassess what you have read so far.

- Horses communicate with each other via a combination of body language, sound and touch
- Your horse can read your body language all the time
- If while out on a hack your horse is frightened by something in the hedge, your best course of action is not to whip him on, but to get off and lead him past

- Your horse should see you as someone he can always trust and respect
- A horse is ready to flee when his limbs are underneath him and his head and tail carriage is high
- A horse may lay his ears back as a sign of aggression, but also because he wants to protect his ears from injury
- Before they kick, horses issue certain obvious warnings via their eyes, facial expressions, and voices; they will also present their hindquarters to you
- It is normal for young horses to investigate everything with their mouths and feet
- Using a windsucking collar is useless as it helps to increase the horse's stress level

3 FIRST PRINCIPLES

Cast your mind back to your school or college days. Can you remember how you really enjoyed some lessons and dreaded others? What was it that made the difference? Was it the subject? The teacher? The way in which the lesson was taught?

Maybe it was a combination of all these factors. The chances are that everyone in the class would have had a different experience, according to their individual interests and rates of learning.

So it is with horses.

Above: A horse cannot learn if he is worried, frightened or not paying attention. It is therefore important that the handler or rider can recognise the signs of each of these states and work accordingly. You can see from this horse's lowered head, soft eyes and floppy ears that he is relaxed and giving his attention to Michael

Opposite: Trouble with boxing is one of the most common problems presented to horse behaviourists

- Strive for a 50/50 balance in your partnership with your horse
- Work in the centre of the 'middle ground'
- Gaining respect and attention is essential before any work can be done

If you want to build a house you have to spend time, money and effort on getting the foundations right. If you neglect this area, your house will subside or collapse. Apply this line of thinking to the training of the horse. Spend time effectively at the start of the horse's life and he will give you fewer problems in the future. Imagine if every horse received a good, solid initial education, so that he:

- goes forwards and stops when asked, without resistance;
- goes backwards or sideways whenever the rider asks;
- is accustomed to and not at all worried by traffic, ditches, barking dogs, people with umbrellas, going across wooden bridges or into narrow trailers – or any other aspect of modern life which we ask him to accept;
- jumps small coloured and natural fences.

Once a horse has this basic grounding he can go on to further develop his talents in whatever discipline he and his rider are best suited to. Many horses are never going to be fantastic competition animals but there is absolutely no reason why they cannot be enjoyable to ride and handle. There are thousands of leisure horses around, and those that have had a good grounding are in greater demand than those that are regarded as difficult.

Whatever type of animal you own, you can start afresh and give your horse a better chance in life. If you do this and you keep your horse, you will have a more pleasurable time. If you adopt the Think Equus approach and then decide to sell your horse he will be more saleable if he has no hang-ups.

The principles of the Think Equus philosophy are listed here and then elaborated in this chapter. By understanding these simple tenets you will equip yourself with a very solid foundation from which to help horses in all kinds of situations, and as a result you will become a better horse person and rider. Take a moment to recap on what you've learned so far:

Self-assessment quiz

1 Why do problems with horses often recur?
- **A** Because horses are far smarter than humans
- **B** Because the trainer only half finishes the training
- **C** Because the problem is viewed from the human point of view, rather than the horse's perspective

2 How do horses view humans?
- **A** As one of their own kind
- **B** As a predator
- **C** As an alien

3 What is the quantum leap that we as humans must make if we are to be successful with horses?
- **A** Teach our horses to see the world through our eyes
- **B** Rein in our predator instincts

and view the world through the horse's eyes
- **C** Live in herds

4 How adaptable are horses?
- **A** Very adaptable
- **B** They find it hard to adapt and that is why they have struggled to survive
- **C** They cannot adapt to changing circumstances at al

5 Four keys to success have been mentioned. What are they?
- **A** Think like a horse, act quickly when problems arise, use time effectively and have a positive attitude
- **B** Think like a horse, don't worry about problems, give your horse time and make

sure you have an attitude towards your horse
- **C** Think like a human, ignore problems, dislike your horse and do everything in a rush

6 Why is the horse's sensitivity to atmosphere important?
- **A** So that he can tell whether you're in a good mood or not and therefore know whether he can be naughty
- **B** Because that's the only way he can find his way around the field or stable
- **C** The horse can sense how you are feeling and will follow your lead; if you are scared, he will be worried too

1) C; 2) B; 3) B; 4) A; 5) A; 6) C
Answers

Key themes

Partnership It is vital that horse and rider work in unison, without either party trying to control the other. Horses can manipulate the movements of their handlers or riders just as riders can use ever-stronger bits and training gadgets to exert control over their horses. Control of rider or horse is the antithesis of the Think Equus philosophy. Neither should have the upper hand, although it may be necessary for the rider to control the *situations* which the partnership experiences.

Balance The term '50/50' implies a perfect balance between individuals in a partnership. This is a crucial difference between the Think Equus philosophy and those ideas which advocate that the rider should always have, at the very least, that extra per cent to give them control. Working in a true 50/50 partnership requires total awareness from both horse and handler/rider. Balance is not a static situation, but one that constantly alters. Crucially, the equilibrium is maintained by minute changes and this is why handlers and riders need to learn to work with horses second by second.

Ethics This philosophy is not concerned with turning problems into battles that must be won. A more diplomatic approach is used to ensure that the battle itself is avoided, and the cause of the battle addressed.

For example, a horse may be afraid to jump a ditch. If the horse were aggressively forced to face the ditch, it is possible that he would become aggressive in return. The ensuing battle between horse and rider would involve violence on both sides, but the problem (the ditch) would not really be tackled.

However, by refusing to allow a battle to commence, the cause of the problem can be directly assessed and dealt with. The fear that exists in the partnership is overcome through empathy, thoughtfulness and reward. It is important to note, however, that the problem is always addressed; a partnership is not allowed to pretend that a predicament does not exist.

Learning processes The ability to function in a co-operative social group is a key to equine survival. Horses do it literally by instinct, but we do not. It is our role, as horse people, to reacquaint ourselves with this technique. The dynamic relationship that exists between horse and rider must be honest, unselfish and unambiguous.

There is also an important place for reflection, self-awareness and unhindered learning. This may be something of a culture shock to busy owners who are already trying to fit a great deal into their lives! Taking time out to reflect upon our actions and to challenge our own assumptions and expectations is essential. However, this is the sort of learning no one can teach us specifically; it must be 'felt' in a sense which is becoming less apparent in our scientifically driven society.

Getting 100 per cent Working relationships exist between horse and rider that do not comply with this 50/50 philosophy and, of course, these relationships can be interpreted as successful. But they beg the question: how much more rewarding could these relationships be?

The middle ground When working with the horse there is an optimal area within which he will tolerate adjustments to the balance of the relationship. Young, untainted horses often have a wide area of middle ground, whereas a 'problem' horse will have a fine line. This is because the latter has usually met a human who worked well outside the middle ground, typically the kind of trainer who gives a horse a severe beating.

It could be said that the area of middle ground determines the skill required to maintain the working relationship. The less ground available the harder it is to achieve balance; the generous nature of most horses means that it is harder, but not impossible.

Understanding this philosophy means that we work the 'middle ground' in a positive and creative manner with mutual respect and attention. If we choose to work outside the middle ground, regard for the other (horse or human) is diminished.

There are no short cuts, or instant answers

We live in a society where instant answers are the norm. Added to this is the attitude we have towards our possessions – much seems to be expendable. However, horses are living creatures with their own complex thoughts and emotions. If we take on responsibility for their welfare then we should give them the time and consideration they deserve. If a horse owner is not prepared to do this then there *is* a short cut – sell the horse!

Responsibility   The working relationship between horse and rider exists within the framework that each individual is responsible for their own actions. In addition, neither horse nor rider tries to take on the other's responsibility. The Think Equus view is 'My responsibility is mine, yours is yours, and we may have responsibilities to each other'.

Dynamic awareness   Individuals and their relationships are not static, but dynamic. It is not enough to therefore presume to know an individual (whether horse or human) because one has a fixed mental picture of their personality. The Think Equus philosophy calls for an active form of empathy, so that the individual is constantly aware of the fluid, ever-changing nature of him/herself and of others.

Setting targets   As a result, targets for achievement are not rigidly set, but also remain fluid: it is hoped that certain goals are achieved, but the progress is not linear. The goals can change, as can the way of achieving them. This flexibility is vital as every horse is an individual, with his own unique experience of the world, and needs to be handled sympathetically.

Collaboration and trust   Dynamic awareness brings with it a sense of closeness, as the changing needs of the other are fully valued. Therefore the progressing relationship between individuals becomes increasingly collaborative. Moreover, the respect for the nature of the individual and the constant 'reading' of each other builds trust.

Let go of your ego   If you think about your experiences at school, in the workplace, on the sports field, at the livery yard or at a show, you can no doubt recall countless examples where people have allowed their egos to run away with them. This usually means that someone else loses out – perhaps, as a result, the latter feels undermined, undervalued or simply upset. However, through thought and awareness many 'I win, you lose' situations can be turned into 'win, win' for both parties. This is what you want to achieve with

your horse. You will create unnecessary obstacles if you refuse to put your ego to one side.

Now that you have an overview of the basic principles and values underlying Think Equus it is time to go into further detail.

The real problems that exist between people and horses are often masked by the symptoms. In other words it's not enough to deal with the symptoms alone; you have to find the cause. If you do not do this things cannot improve for the long term; you are simply whitewashing over the issue, and the problem will return in a short while.

People often ask Michael how he deals with a specific problem like a rearing horse. There is no simple answer. It's so tied up with the way in which the person perceives their horse that giving them a technique to deal with a specific problem is not enough. The rider has to learn to see why that horse has chosen to rear and make the necessary changes in the relationship early enough so that the rearing doesn't occur. This is the key.

Another common question is 'What do I do when my horse bites my arm?' When Michael replies 'Rub your arm until the pain goes away and get a better relationship so that it doesn't happen again', people think he's being rude or evading the question; but it's too late to do anything once the problem has occurred.

It's a simple principle to understand, but knowing how to apply it in the many different situations that arise with horses is difficult. However, it all comes down to one thing, and that's the relationship. If it's good – respectful, attentive, willing, and so on – a horse will feel secure enough not to rear or buck out of fear or disrespect.

The 'big three' principles are the 50/50 partnership, balance, and the middle ground.

The 50/50 partnership

The best horsemanship ever is a 50/50 partnership and this is what we should strive for every second we are working around our horses. In a partnership each party does his or her bit for the benefit of the whole. You help each other out whenever necessary because you recognise the value of each other's input. In a genuine partnership, each party gives 100 per cent, and there is

■ Here Michael is giving the horse responsibility for himself; he is giving the horse time to assess the new situation and work out for himself if everything is all right

no resentment or exploitation between the two players. It's a relationship founded on respect and responsibility and each party must work to make the adjustments necessary to keep the partnership in balance. As long as both parties are happy with the deal they get overall, the partnership will be productive and develop.

Horses have evolved to live in groups, and find it impossible to survive outside on their own. They are very sociable animals and put a large amount of emphasis on creating effective interactions with other members of their group. It's important to them. They know their position within their group and they know the position of others. Anything that upsets the balance is addressed instantly by all members.

The big advantage of this is that horses therefore understand the concept of co-operation perfectly before we even begin work with them. It isn't something they need to learn from us, rather something we need to understand and learn for ourselves. We have to learn how to live and work with horses the way other horses would.

THE IMPORTANCE OF BALANCE BETWEEN HORSE AND HANDLER

- The prevailing viewpoint in the horse world tends to be 'You've got to show the horse who is boss' and 'Any battle you get into you have to win'.
- The 50/50 theory proposes that you work at such a level of communication that you never get into battles or confrontations with your horse.
- It's a working relationship where you both understand the importance of maintaining the 50/50 balance and therefore make, every second, the tiny adjustments necessary to maintain equilibrium and keep the partnership alive.

The 50/50 is the ideal situation but in reality it is very rarely realised between horse and human. This is because of the differences between us. However, if we want to be true horsemen and women we should continue to strive for the ideal and get as close as possible to it.

Some people feel they do more for their horses than they get in return. Some horses feel the same. In spite of this, most horses and humans continue to operate quite well even with things slightly out of balance and still achieve fairly good results. But imagine if the relationship was absolutely in balance all of the time, with both giving as much as they could. The partnership would be the best it could possibly be!

Losing the balance

If you expect too much of a horse and he perceives you as being too hard, he will resent you for it. It's as simple as that. The degree of resentment will depend on how hard you've been (or how far out of balance you've gone) and on the temperament of the horse and his previous experiences.

On the other hand, if you are too easy on your horse and he perceives you as soft, he will probably exploit you. This is not a case of the horse being particularly wicked, but just a natural reaction.

Walking the line between being too hard or too soft on your horse really is a balancing act. You continually have to make tiny adjustments, positive and negative, in order to keep things working and balanced, just as you would if you were balancing a ball on your nose. The more skill you have, and the more you observe, the less severe the adjustments you need to make. While 50/50 is the ideal the reality is that we fluctuate from one side to the other of the perfect balance; but that's no reason to stop trying!

The middle ground

Michael firmly believes that there is not a bad horse born. There may be bad horses about but they certainly didn't start like that. Some are easier to get on with than others, but all have some softness in them that can be developed if we know how to do it. The 'middle ground' theory helps people understand how to work with horses a little better.

All horses have an area of tolerance in which you can work with a certain amount of inconsistency without causing any problems to either of you. Provided you work within this area of tolerance (or middle ground), you can be too hard sometimes and the horse won't resent you. On the other hand, you may be too easy on the horse, and he won't exploit you. In other words, the relationship can go slightly out of balance without doing permanent damage.

However, if you work outside the limits of the middle ground, too hard or too easy, too fast or too slow, you will begin to damage the relationship. You will cause the horse to become less and less generous and the middle ground will diminish. If you keep going the middle ground eventually becomes a fine line as you have eroded the horse's tolerance, and at this point he is usually considered to be a problem horse. It can often look like there isn"t a single bit of softness left in him.

'PROBLEM' HORSES

Sadly, there are many 'problem' horses, as it is quite common for people to be too hard on them. It is more difficult to restore tolerance or middle ground into the life of a horse that has been mistreated, bullied or beaten. Horses that have become disrespectful, as their owners have been too soft, are usually easier to put back on the correct track.

How can we avoid creating problem horses? We should always strive to work in the centre of the middle ground, and the size of this middle ground varies from horse to horse. Some horses are born more generous than others and have a larger area of tolerance. With a horse who is less generous and therefore less tolerant there is less room for error.

Gaining respect and attention

Young open-minded horses are real horses with none of the hang-ups or preconceptions about people that you may find in horses that have been over handled or even abused. So let's assume we're working with a real horse.

Start with something small, like asking him to take a step towards you and then give him a rub on the head. Remember to be polite and ask him, don't tell him. You want him to come to you because it's nice when he does and because he wants to please you.

Now step to the other side of him and do the same, one step then a rub on the head. With every step he takes and every rub on the head you give him, he'll get more and more pleased with himself. He'll recognise that watching and listening to what you do and say is a good thing. Make sure you give the horse room to move to where you want him to go – don't stand in his way.

Remember not to ask for what can't be achieved. For example, if a horse is in an exciting environment or is fresh through lack of work, it's unreasonable to ask for 100 per cent attention; ask for 10 per cent and build towards 100 per cent. It's better to unclip your horse and let him burn off excess energy before asking for attention. Any schoolteacher will tell you it's impossible, and even unreasonable, to try to teach something new on the last day of term. If you ask for your horse's attention and don't get it you lose respect. Only ask for what you can get.

But how do you know when you've got this respectful attention? You know because a horse has a very characteristic look when he is listening to everything you say. You'll see him soften in his neck and his head will lower to the height of his withers. His ears will become loosely half cocked back. He'll follow every move you make around him, with an ear or an eye or both, and his whole attitude will be soft and calm.

We are looking to achieve this with as little effort as possible. Think back to your school days – there were some teachers who could command respect without saying a word. Others would shout and be sarcastic and could do this all day long without it changing anything – they were not respected. Gaining and keeping attention, whether it is of an animal or a human, is not achieved through fear or aggression, but through respect, by being fair, firm and consistent, without ever giving in to bouts of aggression or irrational behaviour.

Once you have a horse's 100 per cent attention and respect it will stay with you until the horse becomes tired. So get what you can done in this time, and stop before his attention drifts away.

At the beginning of their training young horses will become tired quickly and it's important not to try to squeeze too much out of them in the early stages, so keep the lessons small. A horse will be giving you all he can but he'll get to a point where he simply can't give you any more. So recognise this and stop there. It is important to realise that attention is a mental thing: understand that your horse's tiredness is mental not physical. You may think your horse has not done much but he's been using his brain.

This attention span will develop over each lesson with your help. Your goal is to expand it without causing the horse trouble. Ease a horse through a learning curve and don't force it. Take your time or you'll end up wasting time.

Sometimes a horse's attention will get distracted. In this case simply bring it back to where you want it. You should never tell a horse he's wrong but just put him right. If you've done something wrong at work it doesn't help to have your boss going on about your mistake; it is far better if your boss simply helps you make things right. The same applies to your horse, so just direct his attention back to where you want it. Being able to get a horse's attention and hold it is the basis for good work.

Teaching and learning

The speed and complexity of the lesson must be adjusted to suit each horse. Presentation of the information in a simple form is important, but equally crucial is the speed at which it is presented. Both have to be just right for effective learning to take place.

Have you ever been in a situation where someone is teaching you something and the information is perfectly simple but coming too fast for your brain to handle? You have to tell the person to slow down because otherwise you know you'll shut down and give up trying. On the other hand, the information may be presented too slowly in which case you'll close down through boredom. The same applies to horses, and this is why it's important that the pace of the lesson matches the pace of the individual's learning ability. The complexity of the information being presented must be neither too easy nor too difficult.

Horses are absolutely honest and will tell you exactly how they are dealing with each lesson at every second. It's down to us as trainers to see what they are saying and how they are learning. Knowing where to pitch the lesson is essential to good horsemanship.

Keep it simple ➡

Your ability to manipulate a horse's movements shows a horse how important you are in his environment. Conversely, the downside of this is that your inability to manipulate his movements can show him how insignificant you are. Therefore you have to make sure you not only ask him to do things that he is capable of, but also things that you are capable of getting him to do.

1 Introduce a smooth, steady feel to get a horse to come to you. If he resists, maintain the feel until he takes a step to release it

2 When he takes a step towards you the feel will be released by him (negative reinforcement). When he gets to you, give him a rub on the head to make him comfortable with you (positive reinforcement)

3 If his attention deviates use the same smooth even feel to bring it back to you

4 When the attention comes, direct it somewhere. Here Michael directs the attention into a walk forwards

5 Reward him so that he feels comfortable. This gives him a reason to look for you

6 If a horse encroaches on your space, back him up away from you

7 When he moves back show your appreciation by giving him a rub on the head. You've corrected him and then rewarded him

continued

8 Make plenty of changes of direction to maintain his attention

9 Once you have attention you can direct it where you need it. Here Michael is stepping back and asking the horse to move forwards and away. You can see the horse thinking and making the adjustments in his feet to enable him to make the manoeuvre

11

10–11 As he makes the move it's important to feed him enough line to allow him to go forwards freely

12–13 To stop that direction of movement Michael takes a step forwards of his shoulder to slow him down and get his attention

13

14 Use the same principles for the change of direction. Open up a space in front, step back at 45 degrees to the horse's shoulder and ask him forwards on the circle

15 Let your horse decide the duration of the lesson. Using this approach places a lot of responsibility on a horse to make his own decisions. One very obvious sign of mental tiredness is yawning

16 You can't teach a tired horse… so give him a rub on the head and finish until tomorrow

15

16

■ This mare is obviously perfectly happy, and ready to move on to the next stage of the lesson

Presumption is the basis of many conflicts. Just because a horse could do something yesterday doesn't necessarily mean he can do it today. In the early stages of a new skill a horse may be inconsistent with his responses, but as he learns to perfect something new he'll become more consistent. Remember that a horse may know what it is you want but just doesn't know how to do it. So give a horse time to work to where he was yesterday.

Think of a new skill that you have tried to perfect recently. You'll recall that you had good days and bad days. The bad days are frustrating but even more so because you know you've done better previously. The frustration is further compounded if your teacher gives you hassle too.

We must accept these fluctuations as a natural part of the learning process for both humans and horses. If we don't make allowances for ourselves we get stressed which makes the possibility of learning even less likely. In some cases we may give up trying altogether. We must therefore accept that this is a natural part of the learning process for our horses too.

Take some of the pressure away and help him when he becomes frustrated.

If you move around your horse and train him with no sensitivity, two things may happen. Firstly a horse gets troubled and nervous while he tries to work out what he's being asked to do. Secondly he may just harden up to you because you talk too loud. For example, if a child has parents who nag all the time, they create a level of tolerance in that child that may be hard for a reasonable schoolteacher to work at. It's the same with criminal justice. Some offenders are so hardened by their experiences that the system has no control over them at all.

We need to keep horses sensitive and we do this by presenting the lesson neither too hard nor too soft, at the level they can deal with. You can relate this to your own experiences at work. Think of the boss who only ever tells you when you are doing something wrong – this makes you feel uncomfortable and insecure. It's very easy for a boss to recognise when someone has

■ **Opposite:** It is essential to read the horse second by second so that you are sure he is ready for the next step. In this way you will avoid a confrontational situation

done something wrong and often an employee knows he or she has got it wrong but does not know how to do it right. They often just require help to achieve what is needed of them. They certainly don't need shouting at, or their mistakes pointed out, yet this is a very common mistake of management.

PUT YOURSELF IN YOUR HORSE'S POSITION

Remember when you've done something good at work and the boss comes in and simply says 'You did a good job last week' or asks 'Do you need any help?' You feel great (as long as it's genuine!). Actually an effective manager will know when you need help and will offer it at the right time – even before you ask in some cases. You instantly feel appreciated and may even work harder to achieve the same recognition. It's a fact of life: we want acceptance and will work hard for it. So if we do something that causes a good response we will do it again. Good horse trainers are the same as effective managers. They just know the right time to help and how much (incidentally, helping too much is detrimental to effective training; but more of that in Chapter 4).

Relate this to horses. So many horses lose faith in the management – that is, us – because when there is something they don't understand or can't do we don't help them out. Instead, we just tell them how bad they are. You have to recognise every little effort a horse makes and acknowledge it.

Horses are so like humans in many ways. We both live in groups that function most effectively as a unit. It's important to each individual to be accepted by the other members of the family group.

What is acceptable behaviour?

Horses have a hard time; when they understand the things we ask them to do, they do it and we call them good horses and accept them. However, when they don't understand and can't do things we ask, we call

them bad horses. They are not being bad; they just don't understand. A horse is trying all the time to be accepted and finds it difficult any other way. Horses hate trouble and do not actively look for it.

It is often quite difficult for people to accept this. If you hear people talking about their troublesome horses you often hear phrases which suggest that the horse has been standing in his stable plotting some horrendous experience for his rider! This is patently not the case; there is a reason for everything a horse does. While the horse's behaviour may be acceptable or not acceptable in our eyes you can be sure that as far as the horse is concerned his behaviour is justified. It's our job as trainers to create an individual and an individual's work that is acceptable to us.

Incidentally, acceptable behaviour is a personal

thing, so don't let anyone tell you how your own horse should behave. It's up to you, as you have to deal with him every day. If you're happy with the way your horse behaves and he's happy behaving that way, so be it. If you can't live with certain behaviour, then go about changing it. Everyone talks about their horses' problems but how many people try to improve things? We believe there is a solution to every problem and always someone who can help. It's not always easy to find that person because advice is cheap and everyone at your livery yard, riding school or club will be quick to give you their own opinion.

Think about any problems you've had and the people who have helped you sort them out. You will remember the people who genuinely gave you sensible advice that proved relevant, and you will respect them.

■ This is a young horse being prepared for long-lining. You would expect her to react to these new sensations in this way. Make allowances for your horse's education and experiences of life to date

Help your horse to find the solution

Horses have problems too and you should aim to be the person who can provide the solution. However, just as your mentor encouraged you to work through your problems rather than just giving you all the answers, so you should adopt this approach for your horse. If you give a horse all the answers all the time he will never learn to look for solutions. Helping someone too much is detrimental to learning, and you should help your horse to develop the ability to look for answers to his problems himself.

The horse, by nature, is not a problem-solving animal. He is programmed and designed to flee when presented with something he doesn't understand. Humans will stop, think and look for a solution automatically. It's a major difference between the species. Think about evolution. Predators work out ways to catch prey, judge distance and speed and, in more advanced cases, work out trapping systems. Flight animals hear, see, smell and feel anything out of the ordinary, and put as much distance between that thing and themselves as quickly as possible, without thinking. They run first and think second, if they think at all; their behaviour is very much a reflex action.

If a horse is to work effectively in the human's environment, and achieve the complex goals we set, he has to work out many things. He must learn to stop and think when a problem arises instead of fleeing. We should work on a level where a horse no longer feels the need to flee and sees benefit in finding solutions to problems. Once a horse recognises this you can develop it to further the training process.

Training is all a matter of levels and we should be able to see exactly what level a horse can deal with and adjust the lesson accordingly. The process should be progressive and smooth.

Getting the job done

You don't have to look too far to see restraint techniques being used in the horse world. Michael can remember being taught a variety of these at college such as twitching, pinching a fold of skin or holding a tail, and these practices are still around today.

There may be a place for these in certain circumstances, but it does seem that all these techniques require a lot of energy and a certain physical ability. Although they may seem to be effective, this is really not the case in the long run. It's a false economy. They're just a quick fix to help you to get on with things in a busy professional yard.

Getting the job done is one thing, but getting the job done well is more important, and this is why Michael has developed, and continues to develop, a way of working with horses that reduces the likelihood of confrontation and so uses less time and energy. He

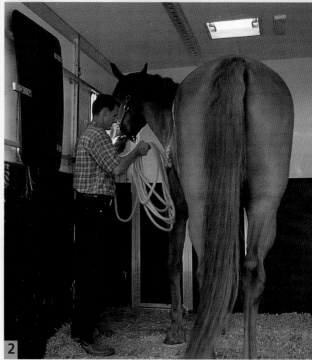

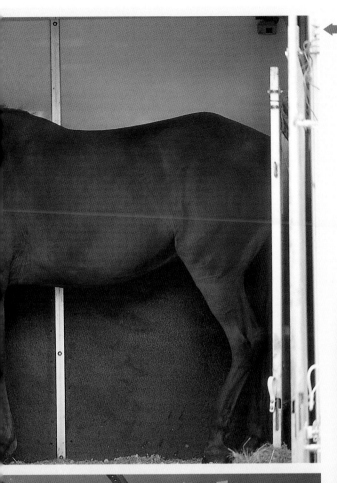

⬅ Horse box horror

This particular horse will load into a horsebox, but when asked to turn panics and rushes out. As the trainer, Michael watches the horse very carefully so that he can ascertain why this is happening.

1 He realises that this is the crucial point – the horse has been moving his quarters over and then simply carries on moving. He is a big, young horse who, as yet, has not learnt to control his whole body. Once he gets moving inside the horsebox, he just keeps going. It is not a case of being wilfully difficult – it is simply that the horse does not know how to deal with the situation. Imagine the havoc that could be caused if 'bully boy' tactics were employed to 'solve' this problem!

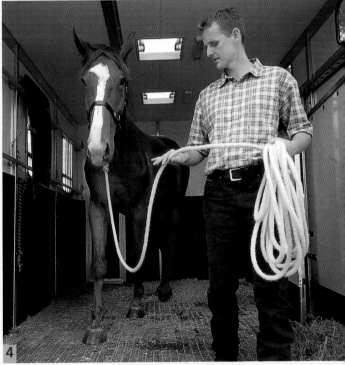

4

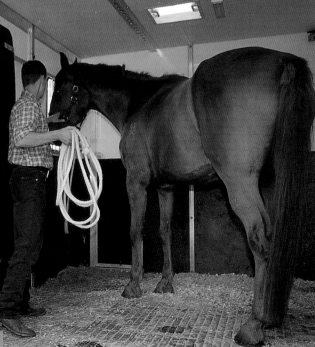

2–3 Michael helps the youngster to turn very gradually, ensuring that the horse has the time to work out where to put his body. This is a good example of working with the horse second by second, as Michael has to be very aware of the youngster's signals – if he reads them incorrectly he could be mowed down by the horse rushing out!

4 By giving the horse help and time to work through the difficulty, the problem is resolved

has learned that a little time invested at the outset to set things up properly, so that a horse can understand what he is being asked, will prevent the horse from getting troubled. This applies, for example, to those common 'horrors' such as shoeing, clipping and loading. This way everyone can get through the day much more easily. After all, horses want a quiet time – and so does everyone around them.

When Michael worked in various professional stables it made sense to get his horses to go nicely because it made his job much easier. There was no point in battling with a horse for the duration of the exercise or every time it needed shoeing. He learned that understanding what was troubling a horse and helping him to deal with his problems made life so much easier for both parties.

AVOID THE QUICK-FIX TRAP

It is easy to fall into the 'quick-fix trap' because of time and peer pressure. Often there is pressure on us to be seen to be making an effort even when we know it's wrong, but this is not acceptable. If it's your horse it's your responsibility, and your peers will be quick enough to point this out when their advice doesn't work. You probably know your horse better than anyone else, so be selective about who you listen to and don't feel pressured. Always remember this: short-term solutions cause life-long problems.

Of course it often takes some thinking about. Solutions are not always obvious and looking for them can be frustrating. But all learning curves require some effort and this is the only way we can develop our horsemanship skills. We can all improve our working relationship with our horses. By thinking through situations and experimenting and listening to the right people, we can develop effective strategies for use in the future.

Using methods of restraint, and any situation that requires force, may get a job done initially but will not actually teach the horse very much. You will find that you'll need to repeat the method each time you encounter certain behaviour, and you'll probably need to use more force each time. It may seem like a quick fix but beware: over time you will escalate the problem, as you're dealing with the effect and not the cause. It is the same route as putting a stronger bit in a horse's mouth to stop him pulling, or battling with him to load into the trailer. One day you will reach a point when there isn't a gadget or a human strong enough to hold him.

Many horses have become hardened through progressive abuse. (Remember it's the horse's perception of abuse that is important.) We all harden up to survive in our own particular environment; if that environment gets tougher, then so will we. It's no different for horses. It is incredible how tough a horse can get, especially when abuse is progressive.

We all have things we don't wish to do in life but we almost always have to do them eventually. We therefore may as well get on with things and work out the easiest way to do them. Horses can learn to think this way too. Our responsibility is to help them. There is nothing worse than having something you don't want to do forced upon you; even if it's not that big a deal it still causes resentment. If a horse knows what needs to be done and knows he has to do it eventually, you can pretty much leave him alone and he'll get on and do it. All you have to do is get him to try and then keep him going.

Ray Hunt is an inspirational, caring horse trainer in the USA. He says 'You've got to get a horse to do *your* thing *his* way'. In other words, there is no point making a horse do something if he doesn't want to do it, because at best he won't do it well, and at worst he'll resent you for making him do it.

When your boss is impolite with the way in which he asks you to do a job, you find it very difficult to do it to the best of your ability. Even when the task is simple it is hard to do it for someone who doesn't appreciate your efforts. Never force a horse to do anything. You have to be cleverer than that; you have to think of a way to get him to do it.

Many horse trainers think that they are doing a wonderful job and that they are getting good results because the horse they're working is doing everything he is asked. So many horses are actually working unwillingly, which is a shame for them and the people who may own them in the future. Such horses are destined to become problem horses.

CHECKLIST Before moving on to the next stage of learning how to Think Equus, take a moment to reassess what you have read so far.

- Horse and rider should work in unison without one trying to control the other, but the rider needs to be in command of things at times so that he can ensure the situation is set up to make it easy for the horse to learn and do the right thing

- The Think Equus philosophy is that a partnership has a 50/50 balance, and in order to maintain this horse and rider must be totally aware of themselves and each other

- Young horses have a broad area of tolerance or middle ground; we can avoid creating problem horses by always working in the middle of the middle ground

- When horse and rider are working together they have their own responsibilities as well as responsibilities they can share

- In Think Equus goals are targets which can change, as can the way of achieving them

- Think Equus requires you to deal with the cause of a problem

- The Think Equus view of a partnership is that it is based upon respect and responsibility on each party's behalf

- Think Equus people believe that horses know how to co-operate with each other

- If you are too hard on a horse he'll resent you; if you are too soft he may exploit you

- If you can manipulate your horse's movements he'll think you're important to him

- You'll know your horse is paying attention to you because he'll be soft and calm and will follow your every move; if his attention wavers you should bring it back to where you want it

- If you want to gain respect from your horse you must be firm, fair and consistent; when teaching him present information simply and at the pace suitable for the individual; always ask him for what you know you can get

- You should aim to be the person your horse turns to, knowing he'll get help

- It's important that the trainer recognises and rewards every effort made by the horse

- By nature, horses run away from problems

- Short-term solutions are great for causing life-long problems

- It is important to get a horse to do your thing his way; horses try all the time to be accepted, and by nature will work with humans willingly

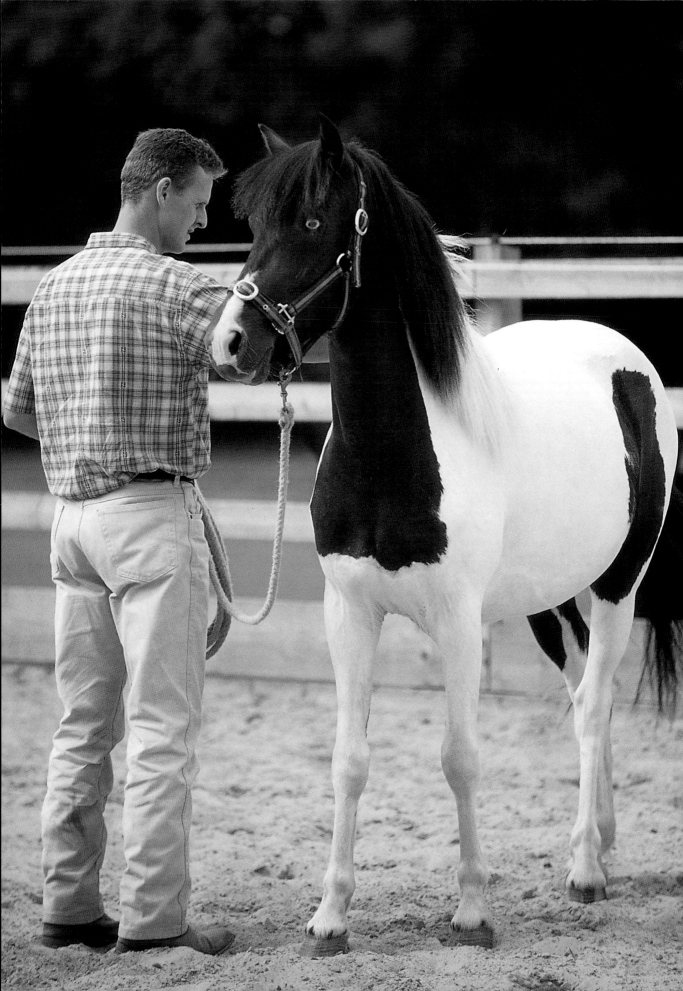

4 TRAINING AS A SCIENCE

Above: Reward every little try from your horse, and make him feel comfortable about what you have asked him to do

Opposite: Always remember that in their natural state horses live fairly simple lives, and may not initially understand our requests

'Don't play with matches' is a phrase heard in many households where there are young children. Despite their parents' warnings many children persist in playing with fire. However, once they have had their fingers burnt, they heed the advice. Experiencing something is one way of learning. Ideally, the experience will be positive rather than negative, and be within controlled conditions.

In training your horse you need to consider how he can best learn so that he is given every chance of a happy and fruitful education.

- Learn to manipulate your horse's space and movement
- Develop a horse's left-brain thinking by giving him small tasks or problems to solve
- Shape your horse's behaviour

Horses and humans both know when

something is right and they also know when it's wrong. The most important point is that we find these things out for ourselves. If there is benefit in behaving in a particular way we will do it. If we can go to lunch early and come back late we will. If our boss reduces our wages accordingly we'll probably modify our behaviour and return from lunch on time. Sometimes we may be unavoidably late due to things outside our control. In such situations it wouldn't be right for our wages to be cut.

People say things like 'You have to show a horse what's right and what's wrong' or 'It has to be black or white'. The trouble is that the world isn't like that. We strive to live in a 'perfect world' where everything is black or white, but in fact spend most of our time moving through the various shades of grey. For example, we would love to have a judicial system with absolutes about what is right or wrong, but the reality is that in order to work our system has to adjust to each individual case and move with the times. What was unacceptable 100 years ago may well be acceptable now, and in many cases is.

Sometimes horses find it difficult to stay within the guidelines we set for them. It may be that they are trying to exploit a loophole, in which case we have to point out that it is not acceptable behaviour. However, it may be that due to the evolutionary differences between horses and humans, they simply can't bring themselves to do what we're asking, in which case we have to help them with it. We must remember that horses in their natural state lead quite simple lives compared to us, and may not understand why we are asking them to do things like jump a fence when there is a perfectly easy way around it!

We must always remember not to take it for granted that we can get on a horse's back and ride. Horses are living, breathing animals, and if we invite them into our lives we must recognise that we have certain responsibilities and we must honour them. We should make sure that a horse is fit, healthy and capable of doing the things we ask. This requires that our horse is correctly shod, properly fed, wormed, and of a reasonable mental and physical disposition for the job he is intended.

On the other hand, a horse's responsibility is simply to be a horse. Six thousand years ago when we began work with horses we saw how much our lives would be improved by utilising their strength and speed. For this reason we should aim to keep horses as close to being horses as we possibly can. They are very capable of looking after themselves. We can do things that they can't do, but they can do things that we can't. This is why horses have been so important in the development of our species.

Obviously both horse and human have to adjust to meet halfway because this is a mutually beneficial situation... or at least it should be. We must recognise the importance of horses to us, and they must see how important we can be in their lives too.

Give a horse a job

In New Zealand, problem horses are often sent to a shepherd for a few weeks. The reason for this is that a horse needs a job to do. If you think about it, a mounted shepherd has a very clear focus when he's moving a flock of sheep from one hill to another or through a valley. His horse has to move where he's asked when he's asked, and at the speed required, or else the flock will divide and get lost.

We can learn from this example. Firstly there is the positive attitude with which the shepherd rides. He knows where he's going and when he needs to get there. He's not thinking about how he's riding particularly but more about where he needs to be and when. This focus is essential for his riding to be effective.

Secondly, the shepherd has to work very closely with his horse and get him to respond when he wants and how he wants. In other words there's an emphasis upon him to develop good feel and timing and the horse's willingness. This involves reading his horse, respect, empathy, responsibility and all those things that make good horsemanship so effective. All good horsemen realise the primary importance of understanding what a horse is feeling and helping him through various situations as they arise.

They also understand that beating a horse will not get anything done and will make a horse unreliable. When you are in the middle of the country miles from anywhere you simply don't want trouble so you want to get the job done as easily as possible. You can't afford to fall off, or get you or your horse injured.

Michael takes every opportunity to move sheep or cattle around or work a rabbit or even a deer across a field in order to get a horse into a job. This serves to give both horse and rider a focus. Eventually you can get a horse to the point where you just have to think about where you want to go; he will feel the slight change in your body and take you there. This is how it should be. You don't want to have to push and pull your horse all day, with every new direction being a battle. Neither of you would make it to the end of the day. If you look at good polo ponies they pursue the ball themselves, in the same way as a Western cutting horse follows a cow on its own. When horses have a job to do they like to get on and do it.

The truth is that if you set a horse a job and he understands what he has to do, he'll do it. Your task is to make sure he understands what he is being asked to do and stay out of his way while he works out the best way to do it. Your only other job is to notice when he needs help and then help him.

Helping your horse

It is important that you consider how you present information to a horse. Clarity and focus are two key words – think of your own work experiences. It is much easier for you to compile a report for your boss if you are crystal-clear about the expected content. If you have lots of different tasks it is easier to prioritise them if you know that your company is focused on,

■ Make it easy for your horse to do the right thing

for example, customer service. When confusion is removed it is easier for everyone to get on with his or her work. The same applies to horses. They want to do their best and it is up to us, as trainers, to make it easy for them to do the right thing.

We increase the likelihood of success if we present our requests or any information to the horse in an unambiguous way. You have to be clear what you want from your horse, what he is capable of giving and also how to get it. You open up the direction of learning that you need and allow it to occur unhindered. Many conflicts between horses and people arise because of our inconsistency in the presentation of our intent or responsibility.

The difficulty in presenting information correctly comes from the differences between horses and people. We perceive situations differently, and we can't always see what a horse is thinking because of it. In order to be effective with our presentation we

GIVE YOUR HORSE SPACE

Horses are very interested in new things and are always keen to investigate. So often people get in a horse's way, either physically or mentally, by:

- Holding onto a horse so tight that he can't actually move
- Blocking him with their body somehow
- Getting in the way of his thought processes
- Starting to hassle him just as he's working something out

It's vital to give your horse the time and space he needs to work things out for himself.

■ Once loaded this filly found it difficult to unload. Michael positions her head to the centre of the exit and then gives her the space to work it out for herself. But she's still stuck and needs help. Michael uses a loop over her quarters to encourage her back feet to move. The quarter loop is not used to pull on the horse but simply to help her to move

need to read the outward signs of a horse's body language to see how he is coping before moving on.

Horses are learning all the time; they will use what works and discard what doesn't. This is why asking a horse to do something for us had better work for him or he simply won't use it. In other words, if you ask a horse to move in a particular direction, make sure you've opened up a space in front for him to move into. You'd better not get in his way, either physically (by hanging onto his mouth), or mentally (by asking too much) or he won't be able to oblige.

Simplicity

Every task, no matter how complicated, can be broken up into smaller more achievable chunks. It may take some thinking about on the part of the trainer but de-structuring a task into smaller more manageable lessons is more productive. Nobody, and especially horses, likes complications in their lives. We want our horses to achieve today so that they come out tomorrow looking forwards to their next lesson. If you make it too complicated a horse will either shut down or become frustrated; either way, learning will not occur.

Speed

It is important that the lesson is not too fast. If a horse can't process the information quickly enough he will get overloaded and troubled. Often when this happens people think that a horse is being bad, but in reality he just can't cope with the speed of the lesson, and it should be adjusted to help him out. When a horse becomes overloaded his behaviour is likely to become more basic, so instinctive actions like kicking, biting, pulling or pushing may occur so that he can escape from trouble. For this reason it is a good idea not to be part of the trouble. We need to understand that this behaviour only occurs as a result of our poor presentation and can be avoided if we continually adjust things to suit the horse.

Finding the softness

Softness in a horse is a willing co-operation that is primarily based on trust. It begins in the horse's mind and its visible outward signs can be seen in the horse's body language, via a relaxed head and neck; floppy ears; soft, slow blinking eyes; licking and chewing; relaxed head and neck movement, and a step forwards

in line with your direction of movement. Finding the softness in a horse must always be the starting point for anything you do together. With some horses (such as those with a generous nature or those who have not had a bad experience with people) it is right on the surface and ready for you to work with. With others, however, you may have to look a little closer. It is always there and it is essential not to proceed until you've found it.

If you can keep that soft willingness in a horse's mind it will come right through into his body, making it easy for you to direct him through the training process, whether it's a step forwards, backwards, sideways or whatever. You don't have to pull or push a horse that has this softness; you simply ask him and he moves because you asked.

This softness must be there at all times. It may be that you're working in a stable, tacking up or mucking out, and you need the horse to move so you can get to his other side. Perhaps you're leading your horse to the field or into the trailer: whatever it is, physically trying to force him through any of these manoeuvres is pointless.

It takes far too much energy, and causes tenseness and resentment in both horses and people. It is important that the softness is there so you can ask the horse and he has the willingness to move his own body for you.

The whole of the training process requires that we can manipulate a horse's movement to achieve our end goal. This should not be dominant control, but more passive direction of a horse's movement so that ultimately he gives to us because he is willing.

When softness is lost
Sometimes the softness in a horse will get lost and be replaced by hardness. This can come from resentment or fear, and is usually a result of poor presentation on the handler or rider's part, either in the past or the present. A horse never gets physically hard except in extreme abuse when calluses form in the mouth. For example, a horse with a hard mouth is almost certainly still sensitive in its mouth, but is choosing not to respond. The hardness people usually talk about in this respect only develops in the horse's mind.

You may not know where the softness has gone, or why, but you should realise that it has and find it again before you go any further.

Manipulating space and movement

Most equine communication is done through body language: they use posture, position, speed of movement, direction of movement, and an infinite combination of all four. It is therefore important for us to understand where we are within a horse's perception with regard to our own posture, position, and so on. In other words we need to be aware of what signals we are conveying to the horse when are working with him.

On top of that we need to be aware and read what a horse is saying back to us because only then can we adjust ourselves to maintain a polite level of communication. This dynamic awareness is essential for effective training to take place.

Horses are very spatially aware and also very clear about what they want to say. What we need to realise is that horses are much better at manipulating space and movement than we are, and if necessary they'll use this skill to their advantage and against the training process. If we are working with a horse and we are not in the right place in the right way he will tell us. If he feels uncomfortable he may run away and avoid our

Manipulating space ➡ and movement

When starting a young horse, it is imperative that we maintain a willing relationship so that he does not use his manipulative skill against us – which is all the more important in a confined space, as shown here. At the same time we must develop our skills so that we can judge distance and speed of movement to communicate what we want to a horse more effectively. This sequence shows how Michael works with a young horse to get him in the required position inside a trailer.

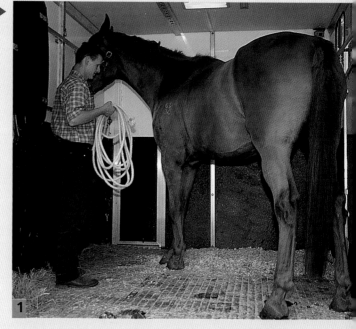

1 Use the coil of rope to move the horse across while simultaneously bringing the head round to you

IMPORTANT THINGS FOR TRAINERS TO REMEMBER

1 Always set a horse a task that is small enough so that he can succeed. He is more likely to come out each day and try new things if he's achieved others in the past. If tasks have been too difficult and the horse has been failing he could become too afraid to try or just think 'what's the point in trying?'

2 Work second by second and adjust the lesson so that it is progressive. All horses learn at different rates and you must know where they are in the process for your presentation to be at the correct level and for learning to be effective.

3 If what you are doing is not working, think about it and change something if you need to. Don't go on doing the same thing if it's not effective because you could be doing more harm than good. Good horsemanship is often about doing less, not more.

4 You can stop a training session at any time and pick up the next day where you left off. Try not to stop on a bad note. Achieve a small success and then finish.

5 Repetition is only good if what you are repeating is of value.

6 Only reinforce the behaviour you want and correct the behaviour you don't want. Get a horse to do something good and then tell him how good he is. Help him succeed. Beware of inadvertently reinforcing the wrong behaviour.

7 Rewards are relative so make sure you understand the horse's value system. Don't over or under-reward. If a horse has been over-rewarded for a small action he may expect to do even less for a big reward. The reward has to be proportionate to the amount of effort the horse is making.

8 Remember the importance of timing. It is important that reinforcement occurs at the same time as the behaviour: not before, and not after.

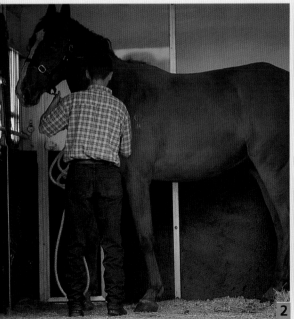 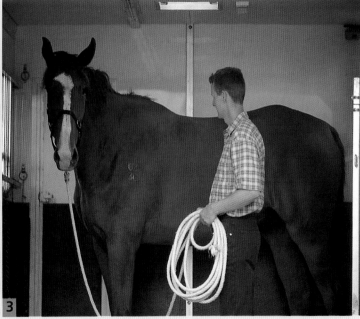

2 Working both ends of the horse together makes him much more manoeuvrable

3 Once positioned, your horse should realise that he must remain in position on his own so that you can move the partition into place

advances and continue to do so until we become exhausted. If the option to run is not available, he may move into our space to back us off our spot, threatening to kick or bite. It's incredible how horses can position themselves quite casually with one or two steps and render us ineffective if they wish to, for example, the horse that positions you up against a wall so that you can't tack up. How many times have you seen someone trying to get a horse started on the lunge and the horse ends up standing still in the middle while the handler runs round trying to get behind?

Manipulating space and movement is something that can be used as a positive influence too. As trainers we will use this to show a horse that we are important in his environment, that we are someone worth listening to and perhaps someone he would like to be with. We can use it to get respect and attention so that we can direct a horse successfully and without trouble through the training process. As an example, any contact with a horse, whether it's direct contact such as through a lunge line, lead rope or another piece of tack, or indirect contact like working within a free space around a horse, is an opportunity to communicate and develop a relationship with a horse.

Understanding a horse's perception of you in any of these situations is key. Only then can you make the adjustments necessary to take the relationship forward. Think of the example leading provides. Stepping a

horse towards you and giving him a rub on the head will be perceived positively because you've led him to a comfortable place. Changing direction and doing the same will have the same effect and the horse will begin to look to you for this.

As you advance your relationship, you'll be able to direct a horse around you and away from you, at a distance during round pen work or on the lunge. It is important to remember that you are directing attention through the manipulation of space and movement: you should not be aggressive or dominant. This is a very powerful tool and must be used responsibly to teach a horse without him becoming frightened or resentful. When you use this tool you must remember not to use it to damage your relationship with the horse.

Teaching your horse to think

One of the main differences between humans and horses is the way that we use our brains. For training purposes we should really invest the time to understand and respect the differences. For example, as humans our brains have primarily developed to rationalise, to stop and think things through in order to find solutions to problems. From an evolutionary point of view this makes perfect sense. Humans are animals who hunt and gather and therefore have evolved to work out what they need and how and when to get it. Horses are different. They are flight animals, and have evolved with quick reactions that enable them to cover a lot of ground very quickly when the need arises.

As a result of their difference in lifestyle and methods of survival, the part of the horse's brain responsible for rationalising and problem solving is not so necessary; it is comparatively underdeveloped because it simply isn't used that much. Horses have developed other equally effective ways of surviving.

In the past 25 years or so, psychologists have really begun to understand how the human brain works. It has been known since Egyptian times that the human brain has a left and a right side that, although connected, can work independently. In recent times, however, the true implications of this have come to light.

■ Pawing the ramp is a good sign. It shows that a horse is thinking about what he has to do. Leave him alone at this point; a few seconds of pawing will result in him making a positive or negative decision. You can then reward forward steps or correct backwards steps

The left side of the human brain is responsible for serial sequential thought. It rationalises using logical progressions rather like the way we understand mathematics, language, scientific analysis, and so on. It breaks information down into small chunks in order to make sense of them.

Conversely, the right side of the human brain has the purpose of synthesising several bits of information into one thought, creating pictures, forming patterns, manipulating spaces, and so on. It is also thought that another use of our right brain is for more intangible concepts like love and loyalty. In brief you could say that the left brain is the logical side and the right brain is the creative side. In our culture there is a huge bias towards left-brain development with right-brain development being hugely neglected.

Look at our education system. Young people who are predominantly left-brain (logical) thinkers are considered valuable because they fit into a logical, sequential structure. Right-brain (creative) thinkers are not so valued because they simply think in a different way and find it difficult to learn in a left-brain education system. The reason some students succeed and others fail is often little to do with the intelligence of the individual student but more to do with the biased influence of the education system itself. For example, rather than trying to teach a subject like French in the left-brain traditional way, which involves memorising words and phrases individually, it could be taught by including the same words and phrases in a story so that a right-brained student could picture their relevance and remember them.

It is now being recognised that individual people learn in different ways and that education needs to be adaptable. Everyone is capable of learning anything with the correct presentation and instruction. Although there has been little research on this subject, Michael believes that conceptually horses are predominantly right-brain thinkers. In their world there is little need for left-brain (logical) thinking but right-brain features like manipulating spaces (for fleeing), forming patterns (mapping), and creating pictures (recognition of danger) could be quite useful in the horse's world.

In reality both sides of the brain have got to interact. Both the left and the right side need developing to unleash more of the brain's potential. The best thinkers in history have been both left- and right-brain thinkers. Albert Einstein was not just a very

---

MAPPING

This is the ability to remember space and how things are arranged within that space. This is useful for a horse so that he can remember a particular landscape, and so relocate good grazing or water, or places that should be avoided. The right brain is responsible for this ability. It deals with visual impressions, patterns and pictures.

The Aboriginal people in Australia are particularly skilled in this area. Living in vast open spaces – as do feral horses – it's important for them to be able to remember certain landscape details so that they can find their way home. These people, like horses, can also see small details from great distances. Their mapping ability is exceptional. Researchers in Australia have recently carried out a fascinating experiment to back up these facts. A board was divided in 16 squares, and an everyday object – a penknife, a pair of sunglasses – was placed on each square. A young Aboriginal girl of about eight years old was given three minutes to memorise where all the items were on the board. The board was cleared, and amazingly she was able to put everything back on the right squares.

Other children of similar age with no Aboriginal ancestry didn't stand a chance. This child had no need of these particular skills in her everyday life: it was an inherent right-brain ability brought about by an evolutionary need. Compared to the other children, she also made more use of the initial time to memorise the board.

Right-brain thinking is the type of thinking required for survival in the natural world.

---

powerful left-brain mathematician but also an accomplished violinist and artist (right brain). Apparently his theory of relativity was stumbled upon while he was day-dreaming on a summer's day and imagined himself riding on a sunbeam to the far edge of the universe... clearly a right-brain thought incorporating left-brain logic.

It is no coincidence that young children are often very good at working around horses; young children are very right-brained. Their logical, rational abilities are only developed much later.

We need to teach our horses to think in a more left-brain (human) way, and we need to teach ourselves to think in a more right-brain (horse) way if we are to create a successful working relationship.

Developing left-➡ brain thinking

Here Michael is extending the lessons taught in Chapter 2, when he worked in-hand with a horse over a sheet of plastic. It is equally important to accustom your horse to new experiences at home under saddle before going out into the big wide world.

1 The mare is doing well, and is ready to move from work in-hand up to ridden exercises. She's allowed to have a good look at the plastic on a loose rein

2 Within a second she's done it

3 This is testing. She hasn't tried it this way before, and she hesitates

4 It's quite tricky and she'd like to bail herself out by taking a step to the left. Michael responds by opening her right shoulder with his right hand and correcting the step with his left leg

1

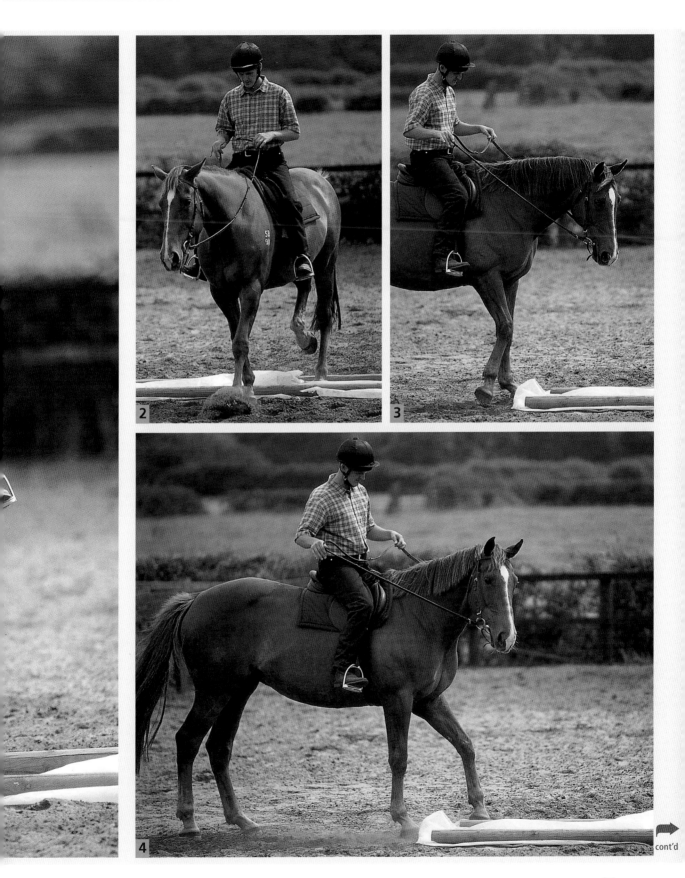

cont'd

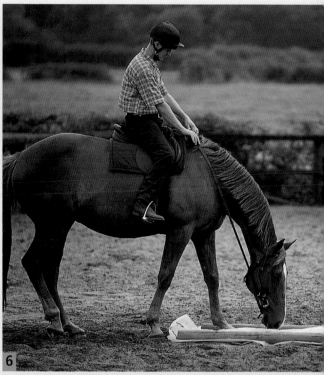

5 She tries to evade to the
right. Michael responds by
correcting with his left hand
and right leg

6 Now she's trying again, so
Michael leaves her alone

7 Another positive decision.
Notice the loose rein, giving
her the freedom to do the
job

8 Michael opens her right
shoulder to keep her on
track. It's been a good
lesson

8

To develop a horse's left-brain thinking we need to set little tasks that cause him to think logically. We literally need to teach him how to think through a problem to find the solution.

A number one rule when developing this ability is to begin with a task that is simple enough for a horse to succeed at. A good start would be something like getting him to make a decision to walk over a coloured pole. It is important that you don't force the decision; it should occur as the result of a thought your horse has had. Just set it up and help your horse so that he finds his own way of crossing the pole.

It is important to keep it simple in the beginning because the horse has got to succeed in order to see benefit in this way of thinking for himself. When a horse recognises this he'll begin to think this way more and more. This is what we need for our future work.

You can further your horse's development by getting him to lead over a piece of plastic (see Chapter 2). You'll have to use your better judgement in each individual case so that you adjust the level to suit your horse at each stage. If a task takes too long you've probably asked him to do too much too soon. Likewise, if a horse gets worried and rushes the task, you should find a simpler one for him.

As trainers, we need to use the right side of our brains to see the whole picture, so that we know where the horse is physically, mentally and emotionally in the training process. Only then can we adjust each training session to effect a good working relationship and successful learning.

JUST LIKE PLAYING CARDS

The process of systematic desensitisation is like building a pyramid of cards. You have to place each layer on top of the previous one, understanding that each step of the process is as important as the first. Care must be taken to ensure that each stage doesn't jeopardise the one that went before it. Each part of the structure has to have the strength to carry the next. The further through the process you get, the more investment you have and the more to lose. One false move and you could lose part or all of the work you've already done.

It is vital to realise that we are not simply teaching a horse to walk over a pole or onto or over a piece of plastic; we are developing the horse's ability to think. Consequently a horse that happily stops, thinks and then walks onto plastic will have sufficient rationale to deal with a small stream, provided he perceives the stream as being a task of similar magnitude to the plastic.

These exercises are not just about getting the job done: it is the thinking that is important. There are many horses competing and some that are winning who get the job done but whose riders have to continually adjust the mechanics of their horses' movement to achieve it. In other words they have to physically make sure that the horse is positioned correctly before a manoeuvre... a bit like introducing a half halt in front of a jump.

If it is sufficiently developed, a horse's brain is quite capable of adjusting its own body to get a job done without our intervention. For example if a show-jumping horse is given the responsibility and has learnt to look ahead to what is needed, he is quite capable of setting himself up to go clear.

The best trainers in whatever discipline recognise this and will continually fine tune this ability and enter their horses only in competitions that progressively develop them mentally, physically and emotionally. These trainers will only intervene in emergency situations in order to help the horse succeed. Most of the time it is left to the horse to do his part (jumping) and the rider to do his part (directing). Show jumping is used simply as an example to illustrate a point that is relevant to all spheres of the horse world from starting and backing youngsters to top-level dressage.

A big part of the Think Equus philosophy is about handing back some responsibility to the horse, which for our purposes requires him to develop more logical left-brain thinking, in order to achieve the things that are expected of him in a human world.

Dealing with phobias

When a horse has a phobia about something, Michael uses a process known as systematic desensitisation to school the horse to accept it so that the training process can continue as normal. A phobia is an irrational fear of something, so working with phobias involves showing the horse that the reality is not as bad as he originally thought.

Let's look at the example of a horse with a phobia of clipping. Many horses suffer from this, usually because of bad initial presentation, which causes fear and results in a flight-or-fight response. You can deal with it in the following way:

1 Initial observation would be to assess the type of horse concerned, taking into account the breed, age and character. During this time take the time to listen to accounts from other people who had attempted to clip the horse in the past. It must be remembered that human accounts are rarely reliable, and should only be used to assess the type of people the horse has had around him. Success is dependent on what happens from here on: what has gone on in the horse's past does not have much bearing on that. This process depends on reading a horse at every second and adjusting your actions accordingly.

2 Having got a horse's attention assess his reaction to a low-level exposure to the clippers. This might involve running the clippers at a distance from him to see what reaction there is. If the initial assessment and the chosen level of exposure are correct, there should be no more reaction than a slight increase in his attention, such as raised head, activity in the ears, and wider eyes. On the other hand, if the reaction is extreme and the horse feels the need to move away from the clippers, and from you, you've started too close and the pyramid has collapsed before you've begun. Knowing what level to go in at is the absolute key if the development is to be progressive.

3 Assuming that you're working at the correct level and that the horse is comfortable with the running of the clippers, switch the clippers off and take a step away. By doing this, you have rewarded the behaviour you want (the standing still) but also got the horse thinking that he can survive around clippers, albeit at a very low level and for a short period of time.

4 Repeating the same process while increasing the level of exposure progressively is the essence of systematic desensitisation. The success of this process is absolutely dependent on the trainer's ability to read a horse's perception. Only with this can a trainer successfully apply a progression that stimulates learning

without fear and the consequent flight-or-fight response. If a trainer is unsure of the level of exposure, it is better that he under-exposes and makes the process slower.

The main pitfall is that of timing. It is important to only reward the behaviour you want. What often happens, though, is that a trainer goes to the horse with the clippers and switches them on. The horse becomes afraid and the trainer switches the clippers off. The trainer began at a level that the horse couldn't deal with, causing the horse to become afraid, and he has inadvertently rewarded the frightened behaviour by turning the clippers off. As a consequence, the horse realises that it is the fearful behaviour that is successful in removing the frightening clippers.

Another pitfall is that people think a horse is just being bad because he doesn't want to be clipped when in fact he is afraid. Consequently they get angry with him which just makes matters worse.

Flooding

This is another method commonly used to deal with phobias in horses. It involves exposing a horse to a high level of whatever he is afraid of with a kind of 'make-or-break' approach. It is rather like locking a person with a phobia of snakes in a room full of them. It either pushes them through to the realisation that the snakes are harmless; or they injure themselves while attempting to escape; or they have a nervous breakdown.

It is actually a high-risk way of getting a horse through a phobia and not recommended. The pitfalls are:

- the horse manages to escape the process before it is complete and is consequently more sensitised than desensitised;
- the horse gets seriously injured as a result of the excess stimulation and fear:
- mental or physical breakdown occurs.

Examples of flooding are stabling a horse with a pig to get him used to pigs, or tying a dummy rider to a horse's back and letting the horse buck until he gets used to that. Obviously flooding takes less skill to implement because you are not required to read the tiny signs that a horse exhibits. Consequently it is often used by less knowledgeable people who, although they may help some horses, often cause more trouble to others.

Shaping

Shaping is a process that Michael uses to train or develop a new behaviour in a horse. He begins with a predetermined goal in mind and then breaks the task into smaller chunks that the horse can achieve and that can be rewarded. To begin with he rewards the slightest occurrence of behaviour that leads towards the predetermined goal. Only when each step is established does he move to the next stage.

Imagine the process of teaching a weanling to hold his feet up for the farrier for trimming. For a farrier to manage this the weanling will need to learn to hold each foot up for about three minutes. Therefore the first part of this process is to get the foot to come off the ground on cue, and this is the first step that we need to shape. As you reach down the weanling's leg, there will be a point where he lifts his foot. It may be that he's telling you to leave his foot alone. However, this is the behaviour you want and so when it happens you must take the opportunity to reward him as soon as possible with a rub on the neck.

Continue by repeating this process three or four times until the weanling is lifting the foot comfortably when you reach down for it. The reaching down is the cue and picking up the foot (whatever the intent) is the required response.

When this is established and the weanling is comfortable, the next step is to try to extend the period of time that the foot is in the air. So the next time you reach down, your aim is to encourage the weanling to keep the foot up for a fraction of a second longer than before. Repeat this three or four times to consolidate that step, and so on.

Continue this process until you have the foot in the air for the required length of time for trimming. It doesn't matter how long it takes or even if you split the training over a few days. What is important is that you are progressing towards the intended goal.

The same principles apply to the introduction of the farrier's tools. You'll begin by using the tools in a gentle way, around each foot, but only for a fraction of a second to begin with. Then gradually you'll progress to the three minutes your farrier will need to get the feet trimmed.

Timing is essential for an effective shaping process. Always end a shaping session on a good note, and you'll be able to pick up where you left off the day before.

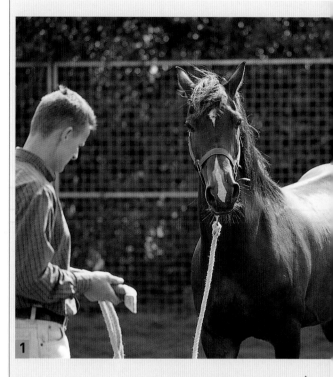

Systematic ⬆ desensitisation

Michael uses a systematic approach to desensitise a horse to a particular aspect of his life that he finds fearful. This process absolutely relies on the ability of the trainer to observe the horse at every second so that he knows exactly how he is dealing with each step. The trainer needs to read a horse so that the horse is never over-exposed; instead there is a progressive acceptance and understanding of the situation.

1 Michael has the clippers running but at a distance (about 6ft/1.8m) from the horse so that he can assess his reaction. By using systematic desensitisation he can decrease the distance between horse and clippers until contact is made

2 It is all too much and the horse can't deal with it. He moves away, but Michael goes with him. By doing this he is allowing the movement the horse wants, but there is no benefit to the horse because Michael remains at the same distance from him

3 The horse realises that moving away doesn't achieve anything. With the clippers still running (in the left hand) Michael gives him a rub on the neck. You can see by his eyes, ears and raised head that the horse is still worried, but he's working at dealing with the issue now

4 Michael makes contact with the clippers, but through the back of his hand to reduce the vibration. He'll work in this way for a few seconds until the horse's head drops and he becomes more comfortable

5 Now that he understands that the clippers will not hurt him the horse is fine, so Michael can continue onto his head and vulnerable areas

Reinforcement theory

Horses live, think and learn by the laws of reinforcement and it is our understanding of these laws that we use to train them effectively. In the horse's world something either works or it doesn't. If it does they'll use it and if it doesn't they will not. It's as simple as that. As humans we are not that different and so it shouldn't be too difficult for us to understand these principles.

Positive reinforcement In a horse's natural state, if there is a place or situation that he finds comfortable he will remain there. If he loses it he will work to find it again. This place may be an area of good grazing, abundant water supply, or may have a pleasing social aspect. The horse will remember it because of its importance to his survival.

We need to understand the simplicity of a horse's needs so that we can create an environment in which he is happy and wishes to stay, but also an environment in which the horse can learn and develop. To this end we must make sure that whenever we ask a horse to do something we give him a reason for doing it. Luckily lots of things we ask a horse to do are built into his nature anyway. However, some of the things we ask are not, and unless balanced with some kind of reward will not be achievable.

Positive reinforcement is the process by which we make a desired behaviour more likely to occur because of a reward that we associate with it. For example, if you give a horse a carrot when you go to fetch him from the field, he will very quickly begin to associate you with the nice taste of the carrot. This is positive reinforcement. You are making the place that you want the horse to be (with you) a comfortable place for him. He'll remember this and will continue to repeat the behaviour unless for some reason it becomes no longer beneficial to him.

The level of reward should relate to the value of the behaviour being performed. Don't reward too much or too little. Rewards must be relevant.

Negative reinforcement Conversely, if there is a place or situation that a horse finds uncomfortable to some degree he will look to avoid it in the future, and he may work quite hard at this. As before, he'll remember this place or situation because his survival depends on it. It could be something he eats that has a bitter taste and he'll remember to avoid it. Likewise it may be a social

AVOIDANCE TACTICS
What a horse will almost certainly learn from punishment is to avoid the person administering it, and possibly also the place where it occurred. For example, have you ever seen a horse recognise a person who has caused them trouble, then run to the back of the stable or to the other side of the field to avoid contact?

situation causing him to change something in his behaviour to steer clear of the situation in the future.

Most conventional horse training is achieved through negative reinforcement. An example is steering a horse with the bit. The rider introduces pressure to the side of the mouth with the bit and when the horse changes his direction the pressure is removed. His motivation in the early stages is not to change direction but to remove the pressure, which then results in the change of direction. Quite simply, something negative occurred so he changed his direction of movement to remove it. It's the same with the use of the rider's leg. Pressure is introduced to the horse's side and he moves forwards to get away from it.

In simple terms, training with negative reinforcement is achieved by making current behaviour difficult and required behaviour easy. Negative reinforcement is a law of nature, and when used correctly, it is a good thing that is used to steer a horse through the training process. The word negative does however tend to give the wrong impression. You should not cause your horse pain while using negative reinforcement. Obviously there are tools in the horse world which use extreme negative reinforcement and do cause a horse pain, like some of the stronger bits, some use of spurs, and pressure/training halters.

The first rule of using negative reinforcement is to use as little as you need, no more and no less. An understanding of positive and negative reinforcement, and more importantly their application in the process of learning, is the essence of good horsemanship.

Punishment

This is not a good training aid for horses because it comes after the act has occurred and doesn't tell a horse what it should be doing or how to do it. Punishment just tends to stir more emotions in an animal that already has a tendency to flee, making them more likely to evade us. Often, due to bad timing, punishment doesn't even tell a horse what he did wrong and therefore is not something that a horse trainer should use if he wishes to be effective.

Napping is a good example of behaviour created by punishment not working. Imagine a young horse coming to something he doesn't like out on a hack. He whips round and tries to avoid it and the rider gives him a smack with the whip. Often in this case the horse associates the additional pain with the place and nothing else. The next day the horse decides much earlier that the place where he had the trouble yesterday must be avoided at all costs and so whips round much sooner, for which he again gets a smack.

As this process continues over the weeks the horse feels less inclined to go away from home because he knows there is trouble out there. This ultimately leads to a horse not wanting to leave the yard or even come out of his stable. Eventually he may even become aggressive when he sees somebody approach with his saddle to tack him up.

CHECKLIST Before moving on to the next stage of learning how to Think Equus, take a moment to reassess what you have read so far.

- Compared to humans, horses, in their natural state, have simple lives
- Good horsemen recognise respect, empathy and responsibility
- It is easier for horses to do a job if they are clear about what is expected of them; as trainers we should make it really easy for the horse to do the right thing
- A trainer should know whether his horse is coping with the work by reading the horse's body language
- All lessons can be broken down as required, according to the horse's needs
- Softness in a horse is something you must find before starting any training

- Training relies upon our ability to manipulate a horse's movements
- Horses are spatially aware
- Teaching a horse to think is something that anyone can do
- During training it is important that your horse has responsibility given back to him
- Systematic desensitisation helps a horse to a progressive understanding and acceptance of a situation, and is a way to help a horse overcome phobias
- Flooding is a high-risk way of getting a horse to overcome phobias
- Shaping is a way of developing a new behaviour in a horse
- Most conventional horse training is based upon negative reinforcement

5 YOUNG HORSES

the unspoiled canvas

If a teacher can catch a child's imagination learning is an exciting journey with the naturally inquisitive child keen to take every step. The teacher's secret of success often lies in two factors: making the environment inviting so the child is relaxed and feels secure, and then adding the element of fun.

As a trainer of a young horse you'll need to adopt a similar strategy, as you too will have a young mind to stimulate and educate. How you approach your horse's training will have a bearing on the rest of his life.

Above: It's a good idea to long-line your horse out and about to get him used to different sights and sounds

Opposite: Use a piece of rope to simulate the headpiece of the bridle without the complication of the bit. Notice the horse's soft eyes – she is aware, but not afraid

- **The most important lesson in your horse's life is being taught to lead**
- **Set up each learning experience to maximum positive effect**
- **Basic preparatory work will prepare your horse for the milestones in his life**

Young

Young horses are a real pleasure to work with as they resemble empty canvases. Most of them have not suffered bad experiences at the hands of humans and so have untainted minds and bodies. They are curious about the world and appreciate a helping hand in their exploration of life. Young horses soak up the experiences their trainers expose them to, so providing the situations which are set up are positive, progressive and educational, the youngster's development continues apace. However, if the trainer gets the situation wrong, the young horse can just as easily learn bad practice as good.

The onus is therefore on the trainer to set up the learning situation to maximum positive effect.

Preparatory handling

You can do many things to help prepare a young horse for the unfortunate necessities of life like veterinary treatment and farriery, and training issues and new experiences such as the introduction of first saddle and bridle, long-lining and carrying a rider. Even if you are not going to be involved in these processes, you can still get your horse ready with some simple procedures. If you do this basic preparatory work your horse will find some of the milestones in his life much easier and more acceptable.

The basic preparatory work should include the following:

Lowering the head   The horse will do this naturally when he's relaxed in his own environment, and it is something we should encourage and maintain where possible. If a horse is tense the first thing he will do is go into a state of heightened alertness and raise his head. This can make him very difficult to work with, especially when it comes to putting on a halter or bridle.

Firstly you need to get your horse comfortable when close to people. Rubbing his forehead and up around his neck will show him that there is social benefit in being around someone. This action feels comfortable to a horse, causing him to relax and lower his head and neck automatically, and it's worth spending a few short sessions over several days working on this state of relaxation. You'll see his eyes go soft and his ears will be floppy.

When Michael first met Soul Rebel (stable name Tyrone) the horse was just five years old. He was a Trakehner by the renowned dressage stallion Vatout, bred for dressage, and with the most beautiful paces. His breeder was a lady who thought the world of her horses and wanted nothing but the best for this new addition to her family.

Tyrone was a highly intelligent horse who learned fast and adapted quickly to his new environment. He was a mischievous foal with a very playful outlook and would have fun even if it meant overstepping the rules. As time went on this little colt's personality grew larger than ever. He became more and more opinionated and often expressed his own ideas about how he'd like to live. Although the breeder thought the world of him he became too unruly and a bit of a liability. She would often recruit her son to handle him because, although he didn't know much about horses, he was much bigger and stronger than she and could use his strength to get the job done.

The little colt grew bigger and stronger, and by the age of two his behaviour had become unmanageable. The breeder decided that enough was enough and although it was a difficult decision for her to make, Tyrone was going to have to go. He was sold.

His new owner was an experienced dressage rider who spotted his potential. Although he was only two years old with awful manners, he had a good chance of growing into a nice horse with the right education.

Tyrone was handled regularly over the next 12 months as the new owner sought to improve his manners. He did improve, and when he had just turned three, he was backed and lightly ridden away. This was to be the beginning of his career as a dressage horse. The new owner kept him entire as it had always been her dream to produce, train and ride a top-class dressage stallion.

As time went by and the pressures of training became more demanding, Tyrone decided that he really preferred his own time in the field rather than dressage. He remembered that if he showed disapproval of something with enough conviction he usually got his own way and wouldn't have to do it. Now three-and-a-half, and much bigger and stronger, he started to make his feelings known. He began with little objections like stopping while being led, barging and refusing to lunge. Over time he progressed to throwing full-blown tantrums, bucking, rearing and even throwing himself on the ground. As soon as he decided he wasn't going to do something, no matter how basic, he would say no.

Tyrone was becoming dangerous again. The new owner wanted to hack him because she thought this might sweeten him up. But she didn't really feel she could trust him enough and she was not sure what to do next.

After some deliberation and following veterinary advice, she came to a decision to have Tyrone gelded as there was a chance that this might have calmed him down. It meant giving up her dream of having her dressage stallion but Tyrone was no good as he was. At least by gelding him he had a chance. So Tyrone was gelded and did improve slightly, for a while, but then it all happened again. The owner decided the best thing to do was to give him a change of scene and let another professional dressage trainer have a go with him.

She sent Tyrone away, hoping that with a few weeks of consistent discipline he would be returned to her as a reformed character. After some time in his new surroundings, Tyrone hadn't learned much more about dressage but had learned a good deal about how strong he was and how effective he could be if he had to. The new people were much tougher on him than anyone had ever been in his life before, but instead of complying with their wishes Tyrone had come out fighting and met them with everything they'd thrown at him.

The owner decided to visit Tyrone to see how he was getting on. When she got there she was not prepared for what she saw. He had degenerated into a horse that had become so aggressive that nobody wanted to have anything to do with him. You were literally taking your life into your own hands if you went into his stable. Even if you managed to tack him up he would buck you off.

The owner was devastated. Her options were limited. Maybe if she left him a little longer he might settle in and just accept the training. She decided to leave him another couple of weeks.

During this time the reports from the yard became less frequent and eventually stopped altogether. The owner decided to drive down and investigate.

On her arrival she was appalled to find her horse undernourished, with rain scald and conjunctivitis. He'd lost so much muscle tone and condition that he could hardly move. She immediately arranged transport and took him home.

Over the next few months it was a case of getting Tyrone back to full physical health to see if there was any chance of him being a dressage horse. As he regained his condition, the behaviour began to return and the nightmare looked like it was about to begin again. On the grapevine the owner heard about someone called Michael Peace, a specialist with young and problem horses.

When Michael met Tyrone he was really quite a difficult customer. Although he was quite young, he had a very cold and calculating attitude to people. He knew his strengths and how to use them to his advantage. On the other hand, Michael got the feeling that he really didn't like living this way but just didn't know what else to do. This is the way that had worked for him and he'd survived some pretty traumatic stuff in the past.

Initially it was simply a case of asking him to do something small, like taking a step backwards or to the side when asked: just giving him something achievable to work on and then rewarding him with a rub on the head or neck.

Over just a few minutes Tyrone really began to see people in a different light. He realised that he didn't have to do too much at all to get approval. It was amazing to see the relief on his face. No more fighting! This was a much easier way for him to live. He no longer felt that he had to battle with people or push them around.

Michael continued this work over the next few months and Tyrone went from being a horse with an attitude to a young, willing horse, happy to get to work.

Since then Tyrone has become a dressage horse at last, and in 1999 competed with his new rider Claudia Steele at the National Championships at Stoneleigh. Claudia has done an excellent job to continue Michael's work, and now looks like she'll take him further to develop his full potential.

Once you are sure a horse is really comfortable, you can then proceed to work with the head and neck. See if you can move his head left, right, up and down while maintaining the softness. Only ever flex him one or two degrees in any direction. Your aim is simply to see if your horse is relaxed enough to trust you to work and manoeuvre his head. Never try to make a horse lower his head with force as this will cause tension and the head will rise.

Face, ears, poll, muzzle, mouth
Now you can extend your work by rubbing around the ears, eyes, poll, muzzle and mouth. By this time your horse should be relaxed enough to enjoy your contact. On the other hand, some horses can be quite touchy about some of these areas. The key is to take it slowly so that a horse sees it as a comforting exercise and stays relaxed. Don't have a fixed objective in your mind; just let the rubbing of the head extend naturally into these areas.

Shoulders, back, flanks and quarters
As you work along, you can extend down a horse's body through the neck, shoulders, back, flanks and quarters. The same principles apply. Don't impose yourself on a horse. The purpose of this work is to get a horse comfortable to have you around, even near his most vulnerable areas.

■ **Above:** It's sensible to teach a horse to lower his head to a position that's easy for you to work, especially for bridling

■ **Top right:** Young horses are often sceptical about allowing us to handle them around their mouths. Grazing takes up most of a horse's day, and so the mouth is very important for survival; a horse will protect his mouth

■ **Centre right:** Presenting your hand so that a horse finds and investigates it for himself. Don't pursue him; let him find you

■ **Far right:** Playing with a horse's mouth will show him that there is nothing to be afraid of

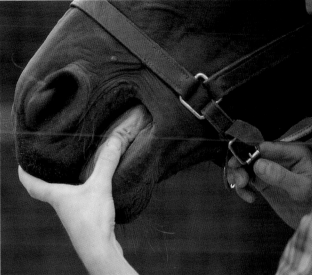

All this handling should be done equally on the left and the right side, and it is quite helpful if you maintain the contact with your horse all the way along each side. It doesn't matter how long it takes, but it is an important preparation that you should try to do as early on in a horse's life as possible. You can actually start touching a foal all over his body a few hours after birth. The important thing is to allow mare and foal to bond before a human starts to get involved with the new arrival.

Legs and feet As a horse is a flight animal, his feet and legs are very important to his survival and consequently he may find it quite difficult to allow you around them. Thanks to the work you've done around his body he should like the contact, and so it shouldn't be such a big step for him. At this stage, don't think about picking up the feet; just see if you can rub your hand down the outside of each leg. If the foot comes off the ground don't hold it; just move on to the next leg. Only when a horse is really comfortable with you around his legs will you ask him to lift his feet. At first, when you ask him, he may pick the foot up and then put it straight down again. Don't worry: this is fine at this stage. You will do the same with the next foot, and as you work around each foot the horse will become more relaxed and allow you to hold the foot a

little longer each time. Eventually you will be able to hold it for as long as a farrier will need to during trimming or shoeing.

Leading forwards, backing up, moving the shoulders and moving the quarters

One of the main things a horse is going to need to know is how to yield to pressure. By nature, horses have evolved to move into pressure. As a consequence, when a horse stands on your foot and you try to push him away he leans into you and stands harder on your foot. However, most of the things we ask a horse to do involve moving away from pressure. For example, when a horse is tied up to a wall and takes a step back, the rope goes tight and the pressure comes into the halter. In this situation a horse that knows how to yield to pressure will step forwards to release it. On the other hand, a horse that doesn't know will panic until the rope or halter breaks and so releases the pressure.

Clearly, it is very important that a horse knows to move away from pressure to release it, and teaching a horse to lead forwards and to back up is a good start. You introduce the pressure and the horse learns the benefit of moving his body to remove it. Teaching a horse four-directional movement like this will be useful for the future, especially when farriers and vets are involved with him.

Halter training and leading

Learning to lead properly is a major lesson for a horse, since we probably spend more time leading our horses than we do actually riding them. However, it is also really important for getting respect and attention and building the relationship before moving onto more complex things. At this point in a horse's career he'll either see you as someone to listen to, or someone to take advantage of, or even be afraid of, depending on how you present yourself. It's quite common for people to neglect this part of a horse's education because it's seen as a necessary but unproductive part of the day, rather like mucking out or tacking up. Remember that everything you do with a horse is important. Every second you are around a horse should be seen as an opportunity to build your relationship and educate him, even when you are performing everyday tasks such as leading to the field.

You can begin the basics of leading when a foal is still with its mother, but most people begin teaching a horse to lead when he has been weaned. Michael always begins in the stable with the first aim being to teach the horse to respond to him when he picks up the rope. The horse should take a step towards you when you ask him with the lead rope. The advantage of the stable is that it's big enough for a horse to take a step away from you if he wants, but small enough for you to work on getting him to face you without having to pull on him. There is no point in getting into a tug-of-war with any horse.

At first when you enter the stable a young horse may take a step towards you, in which case you must give him a rub on the forehead before clipping your lead rope on to his halter. If a horse has not been handled much he may run to the back of the stable. If this happens let him get as far away as he wants to; do not pursue him. When he stops, take a step back away from him, and you'll find he'll turn to look for you. Horses expect to be pursued, so if you don't it gets them thinking about you more. As soon as he is looking at you gently make a move towards him and clip on your lead rope.

■ **Below:** This weanling is having her first leading lesson, and gets stuck. Michael helps her find the space and opportunity to move

■ **Right:** A step towards him is rewarded with a rub on the head

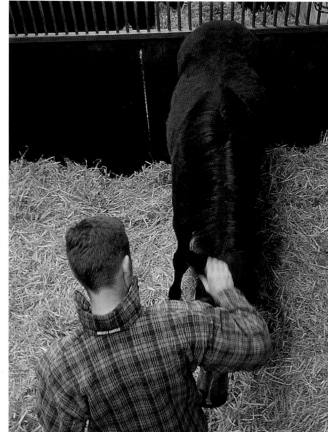

Now you can begin your leading lesson. Walk away from him, and if he doesn't come with you simply let the rope slide through your hands, until you are about 6ft (1.8m) away from him, before asking him again. Giving a horse this extra space in front will encourage him to take a step into the space and towards you. Never hold the lead rope right under the horse's chin and ask him to lead from here, as this is too difficult for him to understand.

If a horse doesn't take a step forwards you know he'll at least be thinking about it because of the space you've opened up before him. Now all you have to do is encourage the movement forwards.

Keeping the 6ft (1.8m) of rope between you and your horse, turn and face him. He'll be looking at you and you'll be looking at him. Take the slack out of the rope and try to draw him towards you. Step sideways, to your left and then to your right, so that you walk in an arc from one side to the other. Your aim is to get your horse's feet moving towards you. So ask with a smooth feel through the lead rope and by changing the degree of angle. You should reward every little step he takes with a rub on the forehead.

Before long your horse will be taking two or three steps at a time and you can begin walking around the stable with him behind you. Try not to think about achieving anything else except getting that movement. It doesn't matter that you're in front of him. This is just the beginning of the rest of his life.

You should work on getting this movement established to the left and right, trying to draw one stride into two or three in both directions. Don't get too involved in the direction you've decided on. Remember it's the forward movement that's important and if you think it may be easier for your horse to go the other way then make it easy and take him there. Once this is established and your horse is moving with you, without being asked, you can think about progressing to a bigger area such as an indoor or outdoor school.

As you walk to the school the same rules apply. If he stops to have a look at something, let the rope slide through your hand slightly as though to leave him on his own. If he's still stationary when you are 6ft (1.8m) away turn and face him and draw him left and right to you. Be sure to draw him to you and not you to him, and don't pull. Give him a rub on the head and then continue.

When you get to the school he may get excited and

TAKE YOUR TIME

The important thing about teaching a horse to lead is to take your time. You'll find the more effective the time spent in the stable, the fewer problems you'll encounter outside. Don't rush things. Be aware of what you are doing. For instance, you do not want to drag your horse along behind you. There should be slack in the line all of the time. He should follow your direction because his attention is with you. If he is frightened by you he will be looking for an escape route. If your lesson is correct a horse will be relaxed and soft with all his attention on you 100 per cent of the time.

You can always tell what kind of relationship a person has with their horse by looking at the degree of softness and attention a horse is giving. If it's lacking on the ground you can bet your life it's lacking everywhere else, especially when under saddle.

try to walk faster than you can manage. If this happens draw him around in a circle to slow the walk down and then continue as you were. Be careful not to get aggressive with him; he is not being bad, just excited. Your responsibility is simply to correct him when he gets it wrong. Never shout, slap him or jerk his halter, as this will just make him worse. If he tries to rush past you simply stop him and back him up, give him a rub and continue.

At this stage, if he finds it easier to follow on from behind, let him be led by you in front. Don't insist on walking at his shoulder and expect him to understand because he won't. This will come later, and to insist on this now will only cause him trouble he can't deal with. Remember he is being schooled in the very early stages of leading.

Soon your horse will become soft: you'll see his head drop, his ears will go loose and he'll be awaiting your changes of speed and direction.

The key here is to start with something easy and progress to the more challenging things later. If you are leading from the near side and want to make a change of direction ask your horse round to the left first. It's much easier for you and for him. To ask for a right turn from the near side is quite difficult. So work on the easy things to get his confidence and your confidence first. If the horse has been properly prepared for each step, everything will work. If it doesn't work it is because the trainer has misread the situation and has taken things too fast. Therefore you would need to go back and retrace your steps, and get the horse happy and secure in his work before moving on.

When Michael teaches a horse to lead he will teach the left turn first, then the stop and back up, and then the right turn last. This is because a right turn requires your horse to slow down or stop so that you can set him up for the turn.

Sometimes you come across a horse that hangs back and leans on your rope. He may have realised that it takes less effort for him to do this than you have to expend in order to get him moving. Once a horse learns that he weighs more than you he may begin to use it against you in other ways, so it's best that he never finds out!

It's important to school this behaviour out of a horse as soon as it occurs. The first thing to try to get a horse's feet moving again is the arcing in front of him, with a smooth, steady feel on the rope. If a horse is really rooted you may need to put a loop over his quarters and, with a smooth, steady pressure, get him moving from there. Never jerk on the rope as this irritates a horse and sets up more resistance. Remember you're trying to help him to succeed, and jerking is something that most often occurs when a handler is angry at a horse.

Instead you should increase the feel on the rope until the first step begins to occur, and then release the pressure as the step comes through. The releasing of the pressure is what is most important because this is the horse's reason for moving. Eventually he'll understand that he should listen for the slightest request to move and lead with you on the weight of the rope.

Eventually a horse will be watching you so carefully that he'll move because you've moved and stop because you've stopped. This is what we want. He's beginning to take up his responsibility in the partnership and work with you on that 50/50 basis.

Handling a horse's feet

A horse's feet are very important to him because horses need to be able to flee from danger and survive. If one or more limbs is damaged a horse's ability to survive is greatly reduced. It's for this reason that a horse will do all he can to take care of his feet and will only allow

Picking up the feet properly

A young horse finds it very difficult to give his feet at first so it is essential that you go about doing this correctly. Don't get angry but give a horse the time he needs. Like so many things with horses, time spent correctly in the beginning prevents problems in the future.

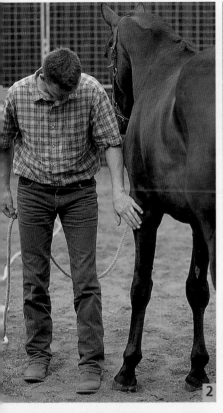
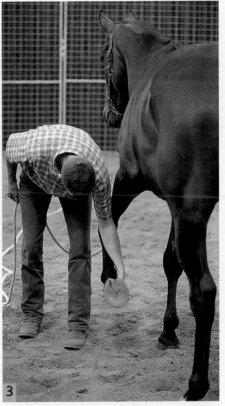
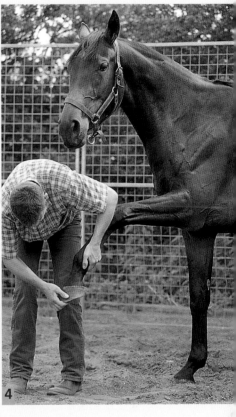
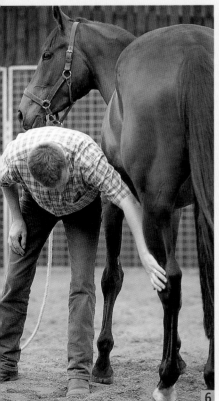
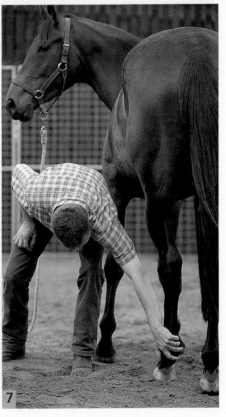

1–3 When picking up a front foot, start high on a horse's neck, continue the contact across the shoulder and down on the outside of the foreleg. As the foot comes into the air, slide your hand to the inside of the foot to hold and support it

4 Once a horse is happy to have his foot picked up and held you can start tapping around it in preparation for the farrier

5–7 When picking up a back foot, start high with contact on the top of the quarters. Keep the contact down the leg, to the outside of the hind leg, and down to the fetlock, drawing the foot towards you as it comes off the ground

you to handle them if he's relaxed and really trusts you. The key is to know how to present yourself so that a horse trusts you with his feet.

If you present yourself incorrectly to a horse, and he feels threatened, the first thing he will do is move away to avoid you. If you continue to hassle him, he may warn you once or twice but will eventually kick out at you to get his point across. You shouldn't think he's being bad; he is simply looking after himself in order to survive. Kicking is a last resort and is a result of you not responding to his earlier warnings.

A very common question is, 'What do I do when my horse moves away all the time?' It is common for a young horse to want to move away when you reach down for a foot. Many people will advise you to hold on tighter to your horse to make him stand still. The trouble with this is it makes a horse more worried and even more determined to move away from you. Unless you are very strong and weigh as much as your horse, this is not very good advice. It is quite common to see people getting angry at a horse because it won't stand still. If you think about it logically, the angrier you get the more a horse will want to get away from you, and the less likely you are to get the job done.

Think about the situation from the horse's viewpoint. Horses are flight animals and need to move when something is troubling them. If you hang on to their feet you are, in their eyes, threatening their life. It is not surprising therefore that they fight more when people hang on!

The secret is to compromise slightly in the early part of this schooling. In other words, allow your horse to move if he gets troubled but only in a small circle around you. You'll continue to do what you are doing, keeping calm, moving with him and directing him round. He'll very soon realise that you mean him no harm.

The ultimate aim is to get the horse to pick each foot off the ground when we ask, and for him to allow us to hold each foot for the period of time that a farrier needs to nail a shoe on. Remember it's our job as horse owners to make sure our horse is schooled to pick his feet up and be absolutely comfortable with this. Farriers are very busy, and it is not their job to train horses.

It is also worth noting that it is going to take time to reach this ultimate aim – it is certainly not something you would expect to achieve in one session. Remember that there are no instant answers but that

effective time invested now will reap dividends throughout the horse's life.

Help your horse to balance Often standing on three legs will unbalance and frighten a horse. Rather than get angry, we must look for ways to help our horse achieve what we are asking. It's important therefore to make sure that a horse is balanced before asking him to lift the foot. Look at how your horse is standing and, if necessary, step him back so that the foot you want is not weight bearing and the other three feet are positioned so that the horse can carry his own weight. This is much easier for a horse, and you are actually helping him to succeed.

Picking a foot up too high also unbalances a horse. Initially you should try to lift the foot just an inch or two off the ground before putting it down again. This way a horse will learn to balance himself. Some horses only have short legs and can't physically lift their feet to the position you've asked.

When a horse gets unbalanced, he will suddenly pull his foot away from you in order to get it back onto the ground. Don't try to hold on to it if this happens. Let it go and then pick it up again, but carefully, so that the horse can remain balanced. If you try to hold on to the foot it causes a horse much more trouble and compounds the issue.

A horse may need to adjust his head position to counterbalance so make sure you leave the lead rope slack enough to allow for this.

Practical tips To pick up a horse's front feet, stand at his shoulder with your leg in line with his foreleg. Place your hand (the one nearest to the horse) high up on the withers and maintain contact as you slide your hand down towards the foot. As you get near the foot a horse may suddenly lift it up. Young horses will lift their feet up and forward. Don't try to hold it at this stage; just be satisfied that the horse has done it. Eventually you'll be able to slide your hand all the way down to the foot and hold it. Remember we are not trying to shoe the horse at this stage; we are schooling a horse to have his feet handled. Therefore every time the foot comes off the ground when you reach down for it, you should reward the horse for his good behaviour.

To pick up a hind foot, position yourself near the front of your horse and reach for the back foot from there. This is a safer position for you. Place your hand high up, but this time on the horse's quarters, and slide your hand down until the foot comes off the ground. A horse may pick his feet up quite sharply at first, but the fact he has lifted the foot is all you need at this stage. Don't try to hold it yet. Eventually you will get to the stage where a horse will allow you to hold his hind foot.

Horses kick with their hind feet so bring the horse's foot forward to you before taking it back to a working position. This will help a horse to balance as well as prevent you from being kicked.

Once a horse is comfortable with you holding his feet it should be a simple transition for him to allow you to hold his feet in the forward 'clenching up' position. The key is to stay calm and help your horse stay balanced.

Often when a horse genuinely trusts you to handle his feet, he will be more confident with you in other areas. On the other hand if you frighten him at this stage, you will lose trust and he will become more difficult all round.

If you are unsure about reaching down around a horse's feet you can use the end of your lead rope to cue the foot off the ground and to check the level of reaction. A progression from this is to put a loop around the fetlock and cue it from there.

Remember to use the rope for cueing and not restraining. You should only introduce a steady pressure to ask the foot off the ground. As the foot comes off the ground the pressure is released.

Starting your horse

There are many factors to consider when starting your young horse. The most important one is whether he is mature enough, both physically and mentally, to begin his career as a riding horse, and this will vary from breed to breed. Most of the time physical and mental development is congruent but it may not always be.

Your horse has to be sturdy enough to cope with the demands of the training process as it unfolds. As trainers we must always aim to make it as easy as possible for our horses to get through each lesson. However, some parts will be perceived by the horse as more demanding than others, and will require an adequate level of both physical and mental strength, for the progression to be achieved. It is our responsibility to know exactly where a horse is in his

---

FINDING A GOOD TRAINER

1 Check a trainer's credentials. Ask about experience, case histories and success rate. See what you can find out on the grapevine. Don't be fooled by formal qualifications, flashy advertising, or a good sales pitch. A good horseman is someone who does a good job with the horses in the yard!

2 Ask if you can see their stables. Horse trainers are often very busy so try to fit in around them and arrange to meet them when it's convenient. Don't judge the place cosmetically but look at the horses. Are they happy and relaxed with good beds and plenty of hay? How are they with the trainer around?

3 Ask if you can see your horse being worked sometime during his education. Don't expect to be allowed every day as this will take up too much of the trainer's time and interfere with your horse's education. All genuine trainers will allow visiting times at some point, so ask if you can make a prior arrangement. Don't just turn up unannounced, as this can be considered impolite.

4 Before you take your horse home a good trainer will want to see you ride him under his supervision. Take this opportunity so that the trainer can talk through what your horse needs and also to see if the horse is at a point that you can continue. Never take a horse home without at least seeing him ridden.

5 Good trainers will be keen to give you a programme to follow. Your success is their success, so ask if you can call for advice if you get stuck in the future.

6 Remember anyone can set himself or herself up as a trainer, so take care. If you are pleased with the service you received tell everyone you can. This will ensure the survival of the good trainers and hopefully the charlatans will just fizzle out over time.

development before we begin, and to only start when the horse is ready.

Generally speaking, horses are sufficiently developed by the age of three-and-a-half years, and therefore most horses are started at this time. However it really does depend on the individual and you must take the time to study your horse objectively to see if he is ready.

How long should it take

Some people think that a horse is done when he has got his saddle, bridle and rider on! Michael's view is that starting a horse is one of those things you never really finish. Owning and training a horse is an ongoing process and it's not actually possible for us to ever get a horse to be as good as he could be. He'll only ever be as good as we can get him; in other words, it depends on our level of skill and desire. This is what makes owning or training horses so much fun. It's a huge subject and we can't possibly know it all, so how long starting a horse will take really depends on how far you want to go.

The more preparation work you can get done, at each stage, the better. For example, mouthing a horse (introducing a bit to the horse's mouth) is essential. Long-lining is also very important. If you can repeat the core essential lessons for a few days at a time, it will help to consolidate the knowledge you've introduced to your horse. Repetition is important, provided you don't bore him. There is another cautionary note: repetition is only worthwhile if what you're repeating is good. Time, just for the sake of time, is not important: quality time is what is important. Day two of a lesson should add to and complement day one – even if by just a tiny amount.

How experienced do I have to be?

If you recall the middle ground theory, all horses have an area of tolerance, in which you can work with a certain amount of inconsistency without causing any problems to either of you. Provided you work within this area of tolerance you can be too hard sometimes or too easy at other times and the horse will neither resent nor exploit you. In other words, the relationship can go slightly out of balance without doing much permanent damage.

Obviously there are some critical stages where an inexperienced person may need to seek some guidance from a professional. But generally speaking you can muddle through and are quite likely to get away with it.

However, you have to look at it from a horse's point of view. He would prefer 100 per cent consistency and would rather have an experienced person taking him through his new lessons. Most people want the best for their horse and will do what they feel is best.

Everyone has to start somewhere and it is not always sensible to throw yourself in at the deep end, especially with something so precious. However, if you do start your own horse, bear these thoughts in mind: seek guidance when you need it; admit any failures when they occur and go about putting them right; and, most importantly, be honest about what your horse needs. You really only get one chance to produce a truly genuine horse. If you're too inconsistent he may resent you for it or become afraid of you.

Facilities

During the starting process you are the teacher and your horse is the student. The place in which the teaching occurs is the school or the classroom. Therefore it's important that you set this area up so that it's easy for your student to learn safely and without distraction. In many ways, young horses are like young children as they have quite short attention spans and get distracted easily. They may get excited or upset and get themselves into trouble so the more you can help prevent this the better.

When Michael starts horses he prefers to work in a round pen for the first few days, measuring $52\frac{1}{2}$ft (16m) across and $7\frac{1}{2}$ft (2.3m) high. The diameter of the pen is important because it gives you and your horse a good area in which to work, but it's not so big that you get lost in it. In other words, you can keep the connection you need with your horse (even when he's loose) and continue to work every second effectively.

The stress of the 'high risk' stuff like first saddling and first riding is greatly reduced if you know you are working in an environment that's safely contained and free from distractions. Your classroom doesn't necessarily have to be that high. It's possible to work in a well-fenced outdoor school, using jump wings to divide the school in half and to round off the corners. This type of improvisation is perfectly adequate, but because of the extreme cases Michael deals with each day he has to be extra cautious.

It is most important to have a good surface (good footing) so that your horse doesn't slip. The horse has enough to think about and does not want to expend any energy or thought on staying upright.

Checking your relationship Before considering getting your horse ridden, make sure you already have a good working relationship. For instance, you should be able to lead him to wherever you wish, ask him to stand and back up. You should be able to handle his muzzle, face, ears, feet and all over his body on both sides. These activities must be achieved calmly, with as little pressure as possible, for it to be a genuine working partnership.

Your presentation should be such that your horse is happy for you to do all these things without you having to resort to excessive force. There is no need for you to raise your voice or your hand to a young horse and it's completely inappropriate to cause a horse pain by using whips or pressure halters. There are other kinder ways of getting your horse to work for you. If you find yourself going along the route of force and domination you're starting on the wrong track, and will need to reassess your work to date in order to find other ways of getting results.

Introducing the first saddle

This can be a traumatic experience for a horse so you must make absolutely certain that your presentation is without fault. Make sure all the equipment you need is available and ready for use before you bring the horse into your 'classroom' for saddling. You will of course need the saddle, the saddle pad and girth. In some situations, for example if the horse is particularly sensitive, you may need to remove the stirrups from the saddle.

1 Have a lunge line or long clip rope attached to the horse's headcollar, bring him to the centre of your working area and stand on his left side facing in the opposite direction, with your left shoulder to his left shoulder. Have your equipment to hand, close to the horse's left shoulder.

2 Hold the horse with your left hand and reach down with your right hand to pick up the saddle pad and place it on the horse's withers. It is important to place the pad well forward.

3 With your horse in the same position, pick up the saddle with your right hand and place it on top of the saddle pad. Now slide both saddle and saddle pad into position ready for girthing.

4 Go to the horse's right side and adjust the girth so that it hangs from the right side of the saddle to about 6in (15cm) from the ground.

5 Return to his left side as before and reach under him for the girth with your right hand. At this point gently ease the girth buckles on to the saddle straps, increasing the pressure until they are fastened. Make absolutely certain that the girth is tight and that the saddle is secure enough not to move should the horse begin to buck.

6 It is absolutely essential that you complete this step without the horse moving forwards. The reason for this is that when a horse moves and feels that girth around him for the first time he will almost certainly buck to try to remove it. Therefore with the saddle secure, unclip the lunge line with your left hand and step back away from the horse. He will almost certainly buck so make sure you are well clear!

Your horse will take a couple of minutes to get used to the feel of the saddle and you should allow him this time without getting in his way too much. Simply keep back behind his direction of movement and encourage him forwards. You want him to feel the saddle in both directions so you may encourage him to change by blocking one direction and opening up the other.

Once you feel he is happy with the experience and has stopped bucking you can go through the process of inviting him to you as mentioned before. The next day when you saddle him go through the same process again and take just as much care as before. He will probably buck again but for a little less time so be aware of this.

Michael also likes to have a wire coat hanger and a narrow 6ft (1.8m) length of cord to hand. These are really for extreme saddling problems but may be needed for first timers if they are particularly sensitive. The coat hanger is used as an extension of your right arm, to hook the girth up to the horse's left side if he won't allow you to reach under his belly. The cord is used as a temporary breastplate to keep the saddle in place for those horses that will not let you girth them up too tight the first time.

Getting your horse's attention ➡

Michael likes to work his horses loose in the round pen but if you do not have these facilities you can 'lunge' your horse. This is not lungeing in the traditionally accepted sense as it is used to check that you have your horse's attention and that you can direct his movement rather than to drill or exercise the horse. Michael will start the movement by sending the front end away first so that the horse's attention goes out on to the circle. He uses his body language to direct and turn the horse, just as he would in the round pen. It is crucial that there is no pulling on the lunge line. Michael also moves on a circle relative to the horse's circle so that he can maintain the communication with the horse.

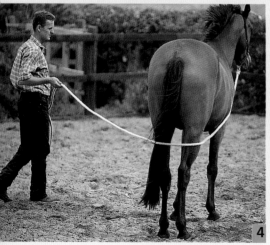

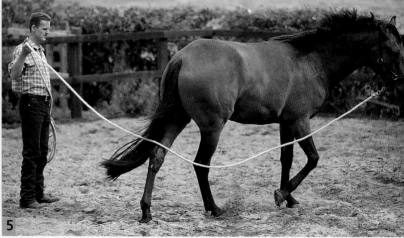

6

7

1 Begin by getting the horse's attention, and then directing him around on the lunge. This gives you an idea of how receptive a horse is, and is also an opportunity for him to get to know you

2 Spend some time getting him used to having the rope up and over his body where the saddle will go

3 Prepare him around his head without the bridle before actually bridling him

4–5 Up to now we have been asking for his attention to come to us, so it's a good idea to do the exercise shown here to get him used to turning away on request. This will prepare him for long-lining

6 To make it easy for him Michael starts work with the roller rather than the saddle. Because of the earlier work Michael has done the horse is quite happy with something on his back, and stands still

7–8 Even though Michael started small, with the roller instead of the saddle, the horse still reacts to it once girthed up. Some horses do nothing with their first girth, but others react quite violently. Do be aware that this can happen, and keep clear. It is very easy for a horse to buck right on top of you by accident

9 Within a minute or two he realises that the roller won't hurt him, and that he can relax

8 **9**

cont'd

10 Move the horse around on the lunge in both directions so that he can feel the roller and see it to the left and right

11 Now repeat the procedure with a saddle. Because of his reaction to the roller Michael has made it easier for the horse by taking the stirrup irons off first

12 Unusually, he bucks with that too, but at least he's going around on a circle this time

13 The process is repeated with the stirrups attached and hanging down

14 Now he's thinking hard and finally working out that it's not going to hurt him. He's still wondering about it, but a few more minutes and he's fine

Long-lining

It's important to have your horse properly prepared before you start long-lining. Make sure that both long-lines are free of knots and fully extended with both clip ends together in the centre of the pen or working area. Invite the horse to you in the middle of the pen. Pick up your spare stirrup leather and move to the horse's right side. Pull the stirrup down and pass the spare leather through the stirrup iron and then return to the horse's left side. Fasten the spare stirrup leather through the left-hand stirrup to hold the stirrups to the horse's side.

Pick up both long-line clips and pass one over the seat of the saddle until it touches the ground. Pass the other clip through the left-hand stirrup and attach it to the bit. Go to the horse's right side, pass the clip through the right stirrup and attach it to the bit. Now you are ready to long-line.

Pick up both lunge lines and direct the horse forwards. As he moves away flick the outside line over his quarters so that it rests behind him above his hocks. Let the contours of the pen guide your horse round and do not pull on the lines.

You can change a horse's direction on the long-lines by stepping out in front of his direction of movement while at the same time gently introducing a feel in the opposite side of his mouth. In the early stages of long-lining you will mostly use your body position to cause the change of direction. What you are looking to achieve is an association between the movement and the feel of the bit on one side or the other.

Continue this process until your horse is responding softly to the bit as his main directional aid.

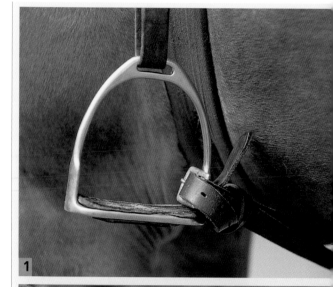

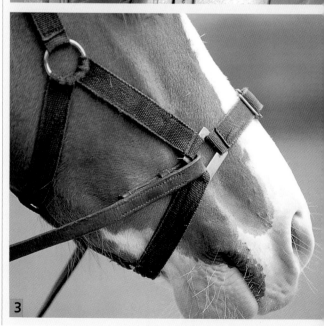

1 When preparing a horse for long-lining, tie the stirrups together under the belly. The long-lines are fed through the stirrup irons to keep the lines in place

2 Fix the reins of the bridle behind the stirrups. They cross over the neck in front of the saddle where the rider's hands will be, and will stop the horse from putting his head down too far. They should not be tight

3 With some young horses you may wish to long-line off the headcollar

4 Lift the saddle pad up into the pommel of the saddle and pull out any trapped mane to make it more comfortable

5 Stretch the legs forward to release the skin from under the girth

6 Throw the long-lines out to make sure that there are no knots in them, and to ensure that they are ready to work with

7 Position your horse at the ends of each line, and pick up both clips together

8 Pass the lines through each stirrup and attach them to the bridle

◀ Preparing for long-lining

Both horse and handler need to be comfortable with the long-lining equipment so that they can concentrate on the job in hand. Your horse must be accustomed, in advance, to lines around his quarters and legs, to reduce the chances of problems or negative incidences. You don't want to start off on the wrong foot; you must give your horse the best possible chance of success.

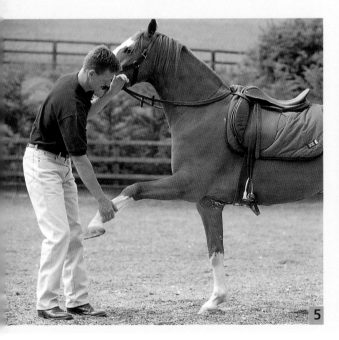

cont'd ➡

The benefits of long-lining

This is important to teach the horse directional control through the bit. With the horse saddled and bridled as previously described these photographs clearly demonstrate the long-lining procedure that Michael recommends.

1 From the near side pick up both reins

2 Step back at an angle of 45 degrees to take up a driving position behind the horse

3 Throw the offside rein over the quarters as the horse moves forwards

4 The key to effective long-lining is to be able to adjust, that is shorten or lengthen the reins effectively. This photograph shows the left hand holding the reins while the right hand reaches down to adjust them

cont'd

5 **6** **7** **8**

5–10 This sequence shows a change of direction from a right turn to a left turn. As the horse moves forward Michael makes his way across to the other side, adjusting the reins as he goes. As he crosses the centre line, note how the horse's attention changes to his left to find Michael. This, as well as the left feel on the bit, facilitates the turn

11–12 It is important to keep impulsion through the turn so that the transitions from left to right rein remain smooth and the horse uses himself. In picture 11 you can see Michael bringing the spare ends of the long-lines across as he changes the rein. This ensures that he does not become entangled in them as he walks

11

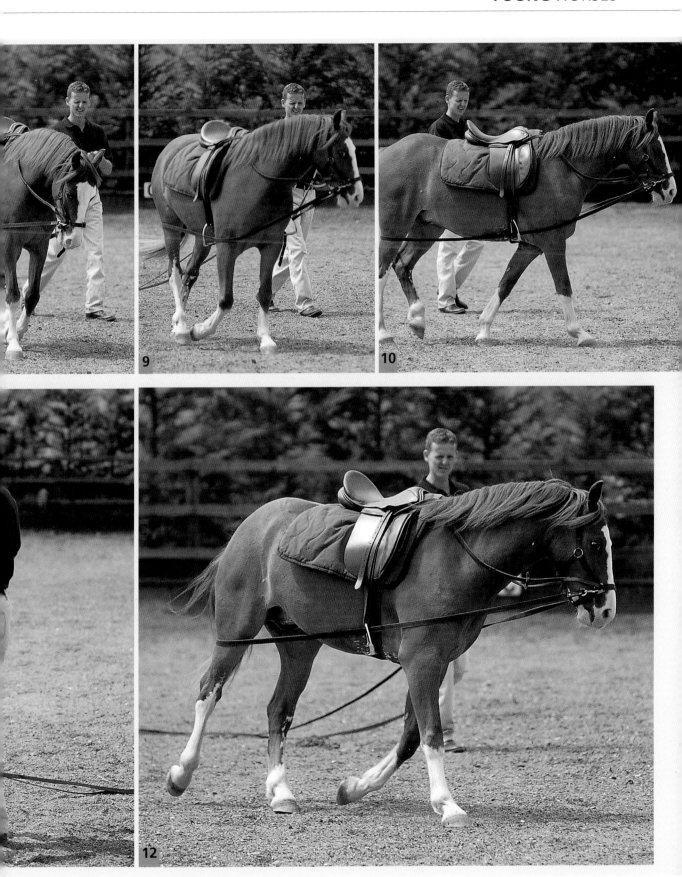

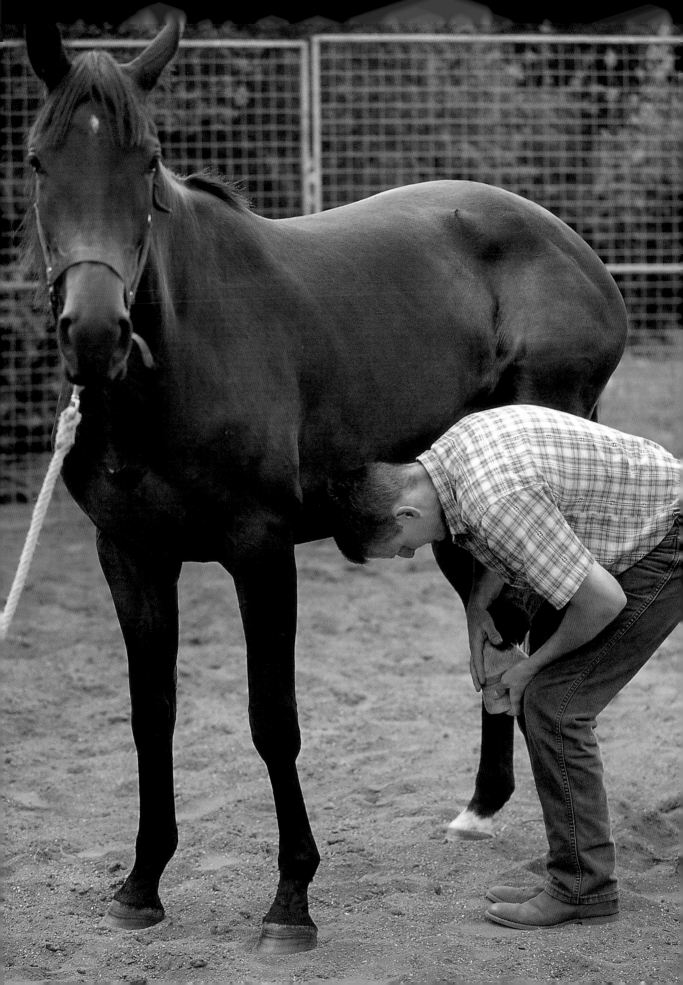

CHECKLIST Before moving on to the next stage of learning how to Think Equus, take a moment to reassess what you have read so far.

- Young horses can learn good practice equally as well as bad practice
- Every second you spend with your horse is a chance to educate him and improve your relationship, and to enjoy him, but also a chance to teach him bad things
- The most important lesson in a horse's life is probably being taught to lead
- If a young horse backs away from you in the stable you should step back and wait for him to be interested in you; if you need to give him extra space to step into, allow at least 6ft (1.8m) to encourage him
- When leading you should hold the lead rope towards the end, allowing plenty of slack

- If your horse refuses to move take the slack out of the rope and move in an arc to get his feet moving
- If your horse gets excited when being led in a bigger area you can slow him down by drawing him in a circle round you
- Teaching your horse to make a right turn when he is being led is difficult so it's the last move you teach
- Never jerk on the rope or headcollar; this can happen when the handler is in a rush, angry, or feeling insecure
- If a young horse lifts his foot and then tries to snatch it away you should let him, allow him to move in a small circle around you and then continue with the job of getting him to lift his feet
- Young horses are easily frightened if they become unbalanced
- Often a horse who trusts you to handle his feet will be more confident in other areas
- Before a horse is started he needs to be physically and mentally mature
- Every day in your horse's education should be progressive and complementary to the previous day
- Ideally your horse would choose a trainer who can give him 100 per cent consistency through the starting process
- Remember that young horses have short attention spans

6 RIDING SKILLS

Learning to drive a car is a landmark in most people's lives. The art of steering, clutch, accelerator and handbrake balance for hill starts and road awareness all has to be developed and mastered. Initial, tentative, short-lived trips soon turn into confidence-giving journeys and suddenly, one day, driving is second nature.

Learning to carry their first rider must be even more daunting for a horse. He has to subdue his natural instincts and learn to carry an unnatural burden that moves around and is often out of balance. Suddenly the young horse has to adjust his balance and carriage to accommodate a rider – and on top of that he has to learn to understand how the rider is communicating with him.

Above: First steps and into trot. It is much easier to allow a horse extra rein in the round pen because he'll never go too far away. It really helps to take the pressure off both horse and rider

Opposite: In time you'll progress to getting your horse out into the countryside. This small gap in the hedge was just challenging enough for this mare at this stage, and a good character-building exercise

- **You have to help the horse move and then associate an aid with this movement**
- **Use a youngster's enthusiasm and direct it in a positive way**
- **Your responsibility, as a rider, is to sit in the middle of the horse's movement and allow the horse to get on with it**

117

Riding a young horse for the first time is a totally different experience. The rider cannot take anything for granted, and needs to understand how the horse moves in order to teach him to associate a change of pace or direction with the cue or 'aid' that becomes part of the communication between them.

Mounting young horses

Part of Michael's pre-mounting preparatory work includes jumping up and down alongside the horse's withers. This will be done well before the first time he gets on the horse. When he mounts a horse for the first time Michael ensures that the girth is tight enough to keep the saddle secure – there may not be the time or opportunity to tighten it once he is on board. Another pre-ride check is to move the saddle, quite vigorously, from side to side so that the horse is accustomed to the movement which will happen once a rider is on board.

To mount Michael takes the reins in his left hand, keeping the inside rein slightly shorter so that if the horse moves he can direct the movement around him and the horse cannot go too far. The loop of the rein is thrown over to the horse's offside. Michael jumps up, aiming to belly over just in front of the saddle so that when he swings his right leg over he is positioned in the centre of the saddle. If you get your belly over the saddle then you end up sitting on the saddle cantle.

Michael finds this a much easier way of mounting. He does not have anyone holding the horse as he finds this complicates matters and can confuse the horse. By

■ These photographs show Michael's preferred way of mounting a young horse, which he usually carries out in a round pen. First he gathers up the reins in his left hand, places his right hand on the pommel and springs up and down against the horse's body to see what reaction there is

Once the horse is happy with the springing Michael makes one big leap and gets his belly across the horse's withers. Notice that he's actually bellied over in front of the saddle; this puts him in the perfect position to swing his backside into the saddle

He places his left foot in the stirrup, and eases his right leg over the horse's back. Make sure you lift your right leg high enough so that you do not brush the horse's quarters. Notice also that Michael has kept her attention around to her left side, as this is where she is used to seeing him

Using a mounting block ➡

Once a horse is comfortable with being mounted by a rider jumping up and bellying over in front of the saddle, Michael teaches the horse about the other ways in which he may be mounted. These include the rider mounting off a fence, from a mounting block and from the ground. The latter is always the last to be taught and is only included once the horse is really happy about being ridden and is used to feeling the saddle shifting. When mounting from a block Michael prefers the block to be alongside a wall or a fence so there is less encouragement for the horse to straddle the block and possibly hit his legs. Whether using a fence, block or stepping up from the ground Michael takes his weight at the top of the saddle rather than on the stirrup iron. This prevents the saddle being pulled too much to one side and the horse being unbalanced.

1

1 The horse is interested in this new and unfamiliar object, and so she investigates it

2 Michael steps to the top of the mounting block while giving her a rub on the neck. It is a new experience for her to see him this high up by her side, and she cranes her neck to get a better view

3 Michael places his left foot in the stirrup, and mounts in the normal way

mounting solo, Michael finds that the horse has only him to think about. A helper can give conflicting signals to a horse and may, through concentrating on the rider, give the horse an unintentional jab in the mouth – not the best experience for the horse!

First ridden steps – walking

Getting the first few steps from a horse can be quite a delicate process. You cannot use conventional leg aids because the horse doesn't know anything about them. You need to find a way of achieving some trouble-free movement and then associating an aid with it. Trying to give an aid to a horse before he understands what it means causes confusion and tension.

Walk is a four-time movement with each leg moving separately as follows:

1 near fore;

2 off hind;

3 off fore;

4 near hind.

To encourage the horse to make that crucial first step, you have to open a space for the near fore to move into by opening your left hand up and out. This causes the horse's head and neck to incline to the left and his weight to shift to the right through his shoulder and over his off fore. The shift of weight onto the off fore makes it possible for him to lift his near fore and follow the direction of his head to take the first step left.

KEEP YOUR HORSE MOVING

If you were on a less sensitive horse and had to cue every footfall of the horse to keep it moving the sequence would be:

1 Left hand up and open for near fore

2 Right leg to bump start off hind

3 Right hand for off fore

4 Left leg to bump start the near hind

In reality you would rarely have to cue every stride like this with a young horse. Most of them are very keen to move once you've got them bump started.

Sometimes this is all that is needed to get the rest of the feet moving in sequence. It's a bit like a bump start. At other times, however, the first step may not be followed through with the other steps of the walk. The horse literally only gives you the step you asked for, to the left, and nothing more happens. This is okay, but does mean that you have to do something to get the next foot to move.

As the horse has moved his near fore already it's almost certain that the next foot he'll need to move will be his off hind. You'll need to use your right leg to give this foot a bump off the ground. The foot should be on its way anyway so it shouldn't need much encouragement.

Be aware that on more sensitive horses the action of the rein should be enough to get the whole sequence of walk rolling. On less sensitive horses, you'll need to use your leg to some degree to support the sequence. It's up to you to know how little you need to use to achieve the movement without getting into a battle or frightening your horse. Please note that you should never squeeze a young horse, especially with two legs simultaneously. This just feels like tension to a youngster and he may have to buck you off if he feels scared.

It's sensible to direct the first few strides around on a small circle. This will eliminate any tendency for a horse to buck because he has to concentrate more on where he's putting his feet. After a few strides you can gradually increase the size of the circle before asking for a change in direction.

Michael always starts a horse's first steps to the left because up until now most of the handling has been done from here. He also mounts from this side since the horse has become quite comfortable with seeing him at various positions in his left eye. Once ridden, making a turn to the right can be quite a shock to a horse as he sees you up on his back with his right eye for the first time. It shouldn't make a big difference, but you will notice some reaction from your horse.

Once your horse is walking, it's important to

■ Getting a horse to swing in walk. Make it easy for the horse to carry you by moving in time with her movement. Swing reins and hands left to right and back again to open up the space for each shoulder. Swing your legs, in time with the swing of the belly, to open up the space for each hind leg to come through. The sequence is: open the right hand and cue with the left leg; then open the left hand and cue with the right leg

understand the sequence of footfalls and how your body should interact with them to help a horse to carry you. The alternate hand/leg movement used for getting the first steps should be continued, but in a less proactive way. In other words, legs and arms should just swing in time with the movement of the horse. If your horse is already walking well you should literally just allow your legs and arms to swing in the following sequence:

1 Hands swing left as the near fore comes off the ground;
2 Right leg swings back along the horse's side as the off hind leaves the ground;
3 Hands swing right as the off fore comes off the ground;
4 Left leg swings back along the horse's side as the near hind leaves the ground.

Using legs and hands in time with the horse's movement like this makes it easier for the horse to carry you and therefore accept a rider more readily.

To cue a bigger stride from a horse in order to increase the impulsion of the walk you would just gradually increase the tempo and the size of the swing of both hands and legs. This works quite simply because both your legs and hands are cueing the horse's legs at the most opportune time, as they are coming off the ground.

Unfortunately many riders employ a simultaneous kick in an attempt to get a horse to give more impulsion. If you think about the biomechanics of a horse's walk, this double-sided kick may help one side of the horse to move but shuts down the other side at the same time. The effect is cancelled out, to the frustration of both horse and rider, and there is no free forward movement.

1 **2**

In the early stages of ridden work, swinging a horse along is so important because it allows him to move as naturally as possible. This enables him to relax and therefore be more receptive to any information we are trying to teach. Any other way and a horse will feel tense, resentful and possibly fearful, and effective learning will be impossible.

People who ride lots of young horses will recognise how important this is. Note that this exaggerated swinging and looseness is specific to the first few weeks of a horse's ridden life. In other words, you couldn't arrive at your first dressage test still swinging your hands and legs in this way. It would look too messy for the judges and they would have to mark you down, even if your horse did a perfectly accurate test.

By the competition stage you will actually still be swinging along with your horse, but by this time the impulsion will be coming so freely from him that your job will literally be just to allow your horse's freedom of movement. As a result you will appear to be sitting still on your horse as he moves, simply because you are allowing your body to maintain its relative position on his moving body.

Good riders do not sit still on a horse but only *appear* to sit still. Their bodies, legs and hands are moving all the time, with each footfall of the horse at whatever pace. If you literally sit still on a horse he will find it very difficult to carry you and will certainly not be able to move as nature intended.

■ When you encounter something on the ground such as white lines, plastic, a puddle, stream or coloured pole you have to manipulate the horse's movement forwards while giving him the opportunity to rationalise each step. You can see that the horse is thinking in the first photograph, and the open position of Michael's left hand is encouraging the near fore forwards. This is followed by the off hind, which has been cued by the right leg. The cues of right hand and left leg are then used

3 4

A good trainer on an educated horse will only give very slight cues with legs and hands: literally a light touch (whether through the bit or from the leg) at the most opportune time, that is, as the foot is coming off the ground.

Moving into trot

Using this swinging rhythm the walk can be stretched out, freeing the shoulders and increasing the activity in the hindquarters until the momentum becomes trot. By building the momentum through walk the transition into trot occurs smoothly and the horse remains relaxed throughout.

The rider should associate a relevant aid with the walk–trot transition. This can be a leg aid, a click or whatever you want. What's important is the timing:

■ **Below:** Here Michael is hassling the horse to pick up in front by raising his hands

■ **Below right:** When she responds everything becomes lighter and easier for both horse and rider. It is the horse's responsibility to carry herself

both the cue and the transition from walk to trot must occur at the same time for an effective association to be made. Remember that it's a perfectly natural transition for a horse to make. As the horse's speed progresses trot follows walk and horses already know this. We just have to build one movement until it becomes the other and then associate an aid with it as it occurs.

The first few times you do this you may find that some breeds will let their walk get quite big and long before making the transition into trot. This is acceptable as long as you take your horse through to the end of the walk so that it eventually, naturally, leads into trot.

All we want at this stage is for a horse to find the smooth transition from walk into trot and to associate an aid with this. We are not looking for collection – this will occur on its own later.

As long as a rider is effective with his timing of the aid and makes the correct association, the transition will eventually occur with the cue alone. This will happen because the movement – trot – and the cue have been paired, and the horse associates one with the other. Consequently when he hears or feels the cue, trot occurs.

The key with all this training is to get the movement first; only by getting the movement can you associate

an aid with it. Because we know that trot follows walk all we have to do to get the trot is build the walk up to as fast as it will go. Once the association is in place you'll no longer have to do this.

Rider's interaction in sitting trot   The trot is a two-time movement with the horse's legs moving in diagonal pairs – near fore and off hind, off fore and near hind – with a moment of suspension between each stride.

As the near fore and the off hind come off the ground together, the rider's right leg should follow the swing of the horse's belly to the left-hand side. As the off fore and near hind leave the ground the rider's left leg will follow the swing of the belly to the right. In other words, the rider's legs cue alternately: left, right, left, right.

On each stride, the hands will open up a space over each shoulder as it reaches forward, that is swinging left as the near fore comes forward and swinging right as the off fore is coming forward. In between the strides – the moment of suspension – the hands will be in a neutral position, neither left nor right, one either side of the withers.

PRACTISE YOUR POSITION IN SITTING TROT

- Stand up straight with your feet shoulder-width apart and your toes slightly turned in.
- Hold your hands out loosely in front of you as if you were holding the reins.
- Now flex your left knee until you feel the weight go into your right heel. If you do this in front of a mirror, you will see that your left hip has dropped to the left.
- Look at your hands; you'll see that both hands have moved slightly to the right, causing your right hand to be slightly higher than the left.
- Now try it the other way and watch the reverse happen. Stay relaxed and flex left, right, left, right in a 'bum-wiggling' motion to simulate the two-time movement of the trot.
- Although exaggerated, this is the action of the rider's pelvis and body for the near hind/off fore stride. Flexing the right knee simulates the off hind/near fore stride.

Rising trot In rising trot, you cue with your legs alternately just as if you were in sitting trot: left/right, left/right and so on. This means you cue as your backside comes into the saddle and again as it rises from the saddle. For example: on a right bend (if you are on the correct diagonal) you'll cue with your right (inside) leg as you rise from the saddle. On a left bend you'll cue with your left (inside) leg as you rise from the saddle. Use of the leg is still just a bump left to right over each stride. Do not squeeze. Your legs should simply be bumping the horse's belly towards the direction of movement he's already taking, left to right, left to right and so on.

If your horse loses impulsion you'll find it easier to bump a bit sharper (still in time and rhythm) with your inside leg as you rise from the saddle. If you are still losing impulsion take sitting trot for a few strides so that you can encourage both hind legs in sequence with a left, right bumping motion.

Never kick with both legs simultaneously to improve impulsion because it won't work. One kick will only cancel out the other and you'll get a neutral response.

Changes of direction in walk and trot

To make a change of direction, many riders of young horses drop their hand down and out from the shoulder towards the direction of the movement. Apparently it's to show a horse the bend! The trouble with this is that the horse's balance falls through his inside shoulder and consequently he falls into the bend. To counteract this you'll see the rider use more inside leg in an attempt to correct the horse from falling in. This often causes young horses a lot of trouble because dropping the hand down causes the horse's weight to fall on to the foot that he is trying to get off the ground. He doesn't need to be shown the bend, but he does need help to lift the foot.

The correct procedure is as follows. Suppose you want a change of direction to the left. It will really help a horse if you raise your inside (left) hand to help him get the weight off the foot that he needs to use to start the turn (near fore). By raising the inside hand, the horse's weight goes back over the off fore and the near fore is freed up to move. It's a simple adjustment, but makes all the difference to help the horse get balanced for the turn.

■ **Top:** As the off fore and the near hind leave the ground Michael raises his right hand to allow the shoulder through and cues with his left leg to encourage the horse's hind leg

■ **Above:** As the stride goes through its cycle and moves back towards the ground Michael lowers his right hand to its normal position and begins to raise his left hand for the next (left) shoulder to come through. At the same time he cues the off hind with his right leg

■ **Above:** Inside leg and raised inside hand as you make a turn. Use the rein to communicate only, not to force the flexion. Maintain the softness from head to tail

■ **Right:** Free your horse up and have him moving freely forwards on a light contact before asking for subtleties like flexing at the poll

■ **Left:** Falling in, in trot: young horses may have a tendency to fall in through the shoulder. Picking up the inside rein, towards the middle of your chest, while the offending leg is in the air, will help the horse rebalance. In addition, drop your outside hand out and down, opening up an outside space so that the shoulder can come through

■ **Right:** Falling out, in trot: in this situation counteract the drift through the shoulder by picking up the outside rein towards the middle of your chest. Also, open the inside hand out and down until you find the balance (degree of bend) you need

If a horse still has a tendency to fall in then open up a bit more space for the outside (right) shoulder to move. In other words drop your right hand out and down, to get the weight onto the off fore, at the same time as raising the inside (left) hand.

Remember you are looking for balance between the left and right side of the horse so you must be careful not to over-compensate to one side or the other. These are techniques that you will use to find the point of balance. Once you've rebalanced the horse you'll return to a normal hand position. The degree of adjustment between left and right hand will depend on the degree of rebalancing that is required.

As a horse becomes stronger and more established in his paces, the less rebalancing you'll have to do. He'll become able to carry himself through the degree of bend that you've asked for. Consequently you will need to raise your inside hand far less as training progresses. If you look at good dressage riders moving their horse through a corner you'll see their inside hand raised a little higher than the outside, simply to communicate the degree of bend they need.

Falling out on a bend is less common and is much easier to correct. Using the same principles, it's simply a case of containing the offending shoulder by

SEE WHAT IT FEELS LIKE

In the early stages you'll need to help your horse change direction, and you can try it for yourself on the ground.

- Stand up straight with your feet shoulder-width apart and toes slightly turned in.
- Hold your hands out in front of you loosely as though you were holding the reins.
- Now open and raise your left hand and at the same time look up to the left.

You should feel your weight shifting from your raised hand to your right foot. This is what a horse will feel and what will help him make the turn.

raising the outside hand. This helps the horse to get the weight off the outside shoulder and back into the balance he needs for the bend.

Using your hands in this way is a communication from rider to horse that seems to be undertstood easily, so reducing the possibility of conflict and accelerating the learning procress. It is not that you are physically lifting weight left to right or right to left but simply communicating to a horse a better way of going. Once a horse feels the benfit of remaining balanced you will not need to correct him at all. He'll find this balance himself.

Adjusting the horse's speed

Young horses may sometimes get a bit keen and run on into their paces in the early stages of their ridden work. It is so important that you do not try to stop

this enthusiasm, but instead use the impulsion towards something positive, like a change of direction. The worst thing you can do is to try and slow the horse down by pulling on both reins at the same time. Often young horses do not understand this aid enough (or perhaps forget it in an exciting environment) and get firghtened by the restriction caused by the rider. As a result the young horse will raise his head, hollow his back and run faster into the bit. If this happens often enough there is a danger of the horse learning that he doesn't have to respond to the bit, and using this to his advantage in the future. On the other hand he may become afraid of the bit.

Our aim is to teach the horse to respond to the bit and not to evade it. Therefore a change in direction in this situation will first of all refocus a horse's attention, which will slow him down, while the turn itself will reduce his momentum. The key is to spot the increase of speed early enough so that you can smoothly redirect it without having to make a sharp change. In other words, it's not about hauling a horse around on a circle to slow him down, but rather calming a horse's thought processes by redirecting them so that he slows himself down.

Once you know how to get the movement you can associate an aid with it as it occurs. For example, you'll use the change of focus and direction to get the horse to slow himself down, and then introduce a light smooth feel through the bit, to make that association with the slower movement.

Other uses of changes of direction

Because of the way a horse learns, you can use a change of direction to reward a good movement when it occurs. Imagine your horse as two horses in one, the left horse and the right horse. What you teach the left horse you have to reteach to the right horse. This is how nature has made them.

■ Use a small paddock and if a horse moves faster than you'd like, direct her round into a change of direction and she'll slow herself down. Don't pull on any horse's mouth — young horses may panic and increase their pace. If a horse wants to move on into canter that's fine. At this stage use your changes of direction to regulate her speed rather than pulling on her mouth. Ride with light, directing reins

Therefore, when you ask a horse to do something to the left and he does it well, you can give the left horse a break by changing the direction and teaching the right horse the same thing. This gives the left side a chance to consolidate the information you've presented while you go on with the right horse's lesson. Once you've finished with the right horse go back to the left and so on. What you are doing is maximising your training session by doing lots of little lessons interspersed with small breaks on each side of the horse. Horses learn better from smaller lessons, and you haven't had to drill one side constantly for the duration of the exercise.

Direction changes also serve to get a horse's attention back on the rider.

> ## REMEMBER ...
> The brain controls everything else, and therefore physically slowing a horse down, without slowing his brain down, will just feel restrictive to him and will result in tension and conflict.

Reining back

At some stage you will need your horse to take a few steps backwards, such as when you want to open a gate while out on a ride. Apart from the practical aspect, reining back is a good exercise in other ways too. Asking a horse to back up adds another dimension to the feel of the bit in his mouth. In other words, when you introduce a feel on both reins to slow down, the horse is not just thinking about slowing down and stopping, but also about the possibility of reining back. Consequently the horse becomes much more responsive to the slow down and stop aid.

When you reach the stage of training a young horse to back up, he should already have a good idea of how to respond to a feel in his mouth. You should already have him turning left, right, slowing down and stopping with the lightest cue from the bit before teaching the rein back.

This is how you'll teach it. Your normal procedure for asking him to stop will be to introduce a feel through both reins and, as he slows down and stops,

you'll release the feel at that point. For the rein back, however, you'll continue the procedure by maintaining the feel even when he's stopped. As he already knows how to yield to pressure in his mouth, he'll realise that there's something else he has to do. He may take a second or two to work it out but if you maintain the soft feel in his mouth, he will step backwards away from it. Obviously, this is the point you release the pressure.

The important thing to remember when teaching a horse to respond to the bit is timing. You must release the pressure as the movement is coming through. A common mistake is to release the pressure too soon or, more commonly, too late.

Cantering

Just like the transition from walk into trot, you do nothing to the trot except build it until it becomes canter. It is so important, at this stage, to stay out of a young horse's way so that he can remain relaxed and the transition is smooth. Once the horse becomes comfortable with the transition you can then begin to associate an aid with the strike off as it occurs.

Canter is a three-beat pace with the footfall sequence: outside hind; inside hind/outside fore together; inside fore; followed by a moment of suspension before the stride begins again. The sequence starts when the outside hind propels the horse up and forwards onto the diagonal pair. After the diagonal pair comes the near fore (lead leg) which precedes the moment of suspension. This moment of suspension is the most opportune time to cue the outside leg, as the sequence is about to begin again. In other words, don't try to cue the canter as the sequence begins, but when the sequence is *about* to begin, that is, just as the outside hind is coming through the air before striking the ground.

If you watch a loose horse canter around a bend you'll see he'll have his head to the outside of the bend. For example, on a left bend you'll see his head tipped slightly to the right. This is to allow his leading shoulder to come through. When a horse is just starting his canter work you need to help him out by tipping his head to the outside in order to free up the leading shoulder. You won't always have to do this, but it will help him in the early stages. On a left-hand bend you would use your right hand to tip his nose to the outside (right) while raising your inside (left) hand up and out to free the left shoulder.

Once the horse begins to move through canter you can follow the movement of his body with your legs, bumping him alternately.

Self carriage – the horse's responsibility

As riders it is important that we understand a horse's abilities and responsibilities. Firstly, horses are athletes and consequently have excellent balance and co-ordination, and are hugely aware of each and every part of their body as it moves through space. If they need to they can place each foot to within an inch of a target. Secondly, their responsibility in nature is to use these abilities and maintain co-ordination, fitness and agility so that they don't slip, fall in holes or injure themselves, and consequently compromise their survival.

These characteristics are all there for us to utilise, which is why the horse has been so significant in the development of human society over the past several thousand years. Horses are fast, can travel large distances, can cover rough ground, and keep themselves balanced. All we have to do is interact with the horse's nature and use these attributes to our advantage.

As riders, our responsibilities are simply to direct speed and direction of movement and develop them within the parameters of the horse's own nature. We don't have to physically balance a horse, maintain pace

or forward movement, or hold the horse together. We must simply sit in the middle of the horse's movement and allow the horse to do what he's been doing for millions of years. In other words we ask for a direction and speed of movement, stay out of his way and allow him to get on with it.

Obviously as riders we will try to develop a horse's natural movement and athleticism to become the best it can, but only within the parameters of the horse's ability and nature. The only way to achieve this is through education, shaping various movements so that they become better examples of a horse's natural movements. Only then will the movement look relaxed, as you'd see in a horse at liberty.

A movement should be communicated and directed by the rider but, once cued, should be the responsibility of the horse to maintain. You can't try to shape a horse's movement physically by pushing and pulling and expect it to be natural and balanced.

Collection

Collection is something that a horse will begin to offer later in the training process. Only when this happens can you begin to shape it into stronger collection and into elevation. It comes from behind and you can get a horse to offer it to you by trotting him up a slight incline. His quarters will have to come underneath him to power him up the hill. This takes lots of energy from a young horse, so don't make it a steep hill and don't go on for too long. You should just wait for one or two strides of collection to occur then reward him by letting him walk. As the back end comes under, you'll feel the front end get lighter which is what we are looking for. Don't try to lighten the front end by pulling on the horse's mouth; collection has to come from behind.

Let a horse give you a few strides of collection and then walk a few strides to allow him to recoup. Then ask for a few more when he's ready. If you go on with too many strides at once the horse will get tired and won't offer them again. You will have made it a tough experience for him and he'll shy away from it. Like anything with a horse, you have to shape it and develop it with small achievable repetitions so that he comes out knowing it is something not too difficult – and something he can do well.

RESIST THE TEMPTATION TO INTERFERE

Too often these days you see riders constantly fiddling with a horse's direction, interfering with pace, balance, carriage and so on. The result of this is a shift in responsibility from the horse (that does less) to the rider (who seems to do more). Riding is supposed to be a more efficient way for humans to get around the countryside. But riders often have to work so hard that it really would be better if they got off and walked!

CHECKLIST Before moving on to the next stage of learning how to Think Equus, take a moment to reassess what you have read so far.

- It's not a good idea to use conventional leg aids when your horse is first ridden because he does not know what they are
- It's a good idea for a young horse to take his first ridden steps on a small circle because he has to think about where he is going
- If you want your horse to move his near fore you can open your left hand up and out
- When applying leg aids it is better to use one leg at a time; kicking with both legs at the same time is useless as the kicks cancel each other out
- Your hands should swing from side to side in a specific sequence according to the horse's footfalls
- The exaggerated swinging and looseness of the riding at this stage is essential for the young horse just for the first few weeks of his ridden life
- Good riders should appear to sit still while moving subtly in time with the horse
- Transitions from one pace to another should be smooth; the timing of your aids is crucial
- The 'neutral' position for your hands is either side of the withers
- If you pull on both reins at the same time your horse will raise his head and hollow his back
- We should teach our horses to respond to the bit
- Horses learn best from small lessons
- It is a rider's responsibility to direct the horse's speed and movement
- Collection comes from the horse's hindquarters

7 OLDER HORSES

coping with their baggage

In our world, the idea that age is no longer a barrier to achievement is an accepted part of life. 'Older' people get back into education, try new sports, undertake travel quests and so on. This often means getting rid of their preconceived ideas and stopping 'doing what they have always done'. They need a willingness to change and the incentive is often provided as they can imagine how life will be once they have moved on.

A horse does not have the luxury of these thought processes and so it is up to the trainer to convince his horse that there is benefit in changing his established behaviour patterns. Horses, like humans, can change, no matter how old they are – and they usually enjoy their new lives too!

- ■ Deal with problems when they are small issues rather than giving them the time to mushroom
- ■ There are no short cuts or instant answers
- ■ Read your horse second by second

135

As horses go through life they may pass through many hands. Fortunate horses will have been started by a thinking horseman and will spend their lives in the company of such people. Sadly, many horses are not so lucky. Even if they have a good start, things can rapidly go downhill if they are sold to the wrong owners. No one intends to have an adverse effect on his or her horse, but often people simply over-horse themselves, take on too much and so cannot cope with the inevitable that follows. For example:

1 A young horse may have been started well and have absolutely no problems with humans. He is then sold on to a less knowledgeable but well-meaning rider. Even the best-behaved horses will soon identify their rider's weaknesses and, naturally, try things on a little. This may just be playfulness on the horse's part but the rider may not be sufficiently experienced to cope. If the rider chooses not to seek help, things often deteriorate as the horse realises that he can 'train' his rider to his own advantage.

This kind of situation is not just the domain of sharp or intelligent horses! We know of many kindly ponies and horses which safely transport their riders on hacks or around the school, but which make the decision when to turn for home and walk sedately back: the riders have absolutely no say in the matter.

However, if the rider seeks help immediately the problem starts, it is often not too difficult to get both horse and rider back on the straight and narrow. But if help is requested later on, further difficulties can ensue. Usually assistance is sought from people who try to paper over the cracks instead of getting to the root of the problem. As these people do not think like a horse they often start punishing him; in the horse's eyes this is unjustified and he may fight back, so the trainer adopts a harder attitude and the downward spiral begins.

By this time the horse, which was perfectly fine initially has, in some people's eyes, turned into a problem horse. The likelihood is that he will be sold on, with his reputation going before him. If he's lucky he'll meet a thinking horseman who can help him. If not, he'll probably end up with someone from the 'show the horse who's boss' brigade and harden up even more in order to cope with the inevitable beating.

Michael has had many such horses in his yard and often it does not take long to find the genuine horse that is lying just below the surface. Horses like an easy life and only turn into problem animals with our help!

2 A perfectly good young horse is sent away to be broken in. However, he is returned without being started and with the trainer declaring the horse dangerous. In such cases the owners usually try other trainers – and the same message may come back. If the horse is lucky he is sent to a thinking horseman who is his last chance and who can find the real reason for the horse's behaviour. If a trainer makes a mistake during the starting process and really frightens the horse he can cause a problem which turns into a major issue. It can be something which to the human appears relatively simple, such as letting go of the horse when long-lining, or having the saddle slip under the belly. However, to the horse this is a serious life-threatening and frightening episode – if you ever see a horse in this predicament you will notice that they are genuinely terrified. An insensitive trainer who then tries to 'sort the horse out' usually produces an animal that will fight and will not tolerate being ridden.

3 A good young horse is started by his owner, who is inexperienced but keen to learn, thinks about what she is doing, and gives her horse the time he

A rider with a few months' riding experience but with a lot of money decided to buy a horse. She bought a lovely, well-mannered young horse and sent her away to be professionally broken. The horse was easy to start but the trainer, when she learned of the rider's inexperience, suggested that the mare was not an ideal first horse. The rider did not want to hear this but she did take advantage of the trainer's offer to have instruction on the horse before taking her home. The rider also promised that she would continue to have lessons. A few weeks later the trainer was told that the rider was having problems, so she contacted her and offered to help, but this was refused. A short while later the trainer learned that the rider had come off the horse and had had the horse destroyed. What on earth could have been so bad as to result in this drastic action? The trainer learned that the horse had simply bucked. It had not even been a rodeo demonstration, just a simple buck, as you would expect any young horse to do. The rider's pride was damaged, she (despite her very limited experience) decided the horse was dangerous and this, in her eyes, justified her decision.

needs. The horse is started and they learn together, each making mistakes, but each being generous enough to the other to find their way through. The combination is never going to be a world-beating force, but they do enjoy life.

Starting off a young horse is a big responsibility, as you can influence the rest of his life; you can affect his destiny for better or for worse. By applying the principles of Think Equus you will be able to help your horse and make life better for both of you.

These are some of the common problems you may encounter, with suggestions on how to approach them. Remember that there are no short cuts or instant answers.

Barging and running off

Older horses may barge you because they have in the past seen that such behaviour works. Examples of this include the horse who pushes his way out of the stable when you undo the

TURN NEGATIVE THOUGHT TO POSITIVE ACTION

Every second you work with a horse you need to know what they are thinking. This way you can redirect any thought a horse is having into something more positive. You can take measures to reposition yourself and adjust your approach accordingly.

door, or pushes past to get away from you when you're leading him. In this situation there is a lack of respect that needs to be addressed.

When you come across a lack of respect in an older horse, you need to give him other things to think about; you need to add another dimension to your approach. Take the horse that barges past you, through the doorway. You must first teach him to move back, away from the door, as soon as he sees you approach,

■ This is a big horse that has learned that pulling away is advantageous and gets him out of things that he doesn't want to do

and only come to the door once invited. Adding this dimension redirects the horse's thoughts from barging towards you to a movement in the opposite direction, away from you.

Initially you may have to be quite strong with your body language in order to get the horse to back away from the door. Once he moves away from you, you should make everything easy for him. He has a place he should be and you have your place too. Now you can walk politely into his space and give him a rub on the head. Remember your purpose is only to redress the balance of respect. You'll do what you have to do to get him to back up, but when he has obliged you must show your appreciation with the rub on the head. He needs to allow you your space and you need to allow him his. Once it's set everyone should be happy. If he wishes to approach politely into your space that's fine.

If a horse has the tendency to barge you when you are leading him, the same principles apply. You are going to add another dimension to the discipline of leading. In this case you'll watch your horse's body language and wait for that negative thought to occur. As it occurs, you have to redirect the thought so that the horse stops and then backs up. When he has backed up you will tell him how good he is by giving him a rub on the head.

BARGING IN YOUNG HORSES

When young horses become afraid they push through you or pull away, not to be naughty but simply because you are in their way. They run blindly over, or away from you, to escape from what they consider to be a stressful situation. If you have done your preparation work and halter training correctly this shouldn't occur. Check your presentation to ensure that you are not causing the horse trouble.

Some youngsters may get cheeky and try to manipulate your position in which case you have to take steps to get things balanced again. It is essential to remember that young horses are very fragile, both emotionally and physically. Don't be aggressive by shouting or pulling them around. If they step out of line for whatever reason, use as little action as is necessary to redirect them to something positive.

You don't want him to feel intimidated by you as you ask him to back up. You're simply redirecting him to something positive so that he sees more benefit in this than in the negative action. Timing is crucial; the thought has to be redirected as it occurs, not before or after. The level at which you work is also crucial: not too hard, not too soft. Remember the 50:50 principle.

Obviously, once behaviour such as barging or running off have occurred, it's too late and there isn't much you can do. This is why it's important to read your horse effectively in the first place. You need to know what your horse is thinking because then you'll be able to see the negative thoughts occurring and can redirect them before they cause you trouble. You'll also recognise the positive thoughts which you can then reward. In addition you will be able to see your horse's perception of you, which will help you make the adjustments to maintain the 50:50 balance.

Behaving badly in the stable

This may include kicking, biting or intimidating humans. Such behaviour shows a lack of respect for the handler or their personal space. The problem is that once a horse has learned that he can behave in this way and manipulate your movements he will continue to do so until he is shown that there is no longer any benefit in his action. See the sections on gaining respect and attention (pages 56–64) and manipulating space and movement (pages 76–8).

Behaving for the vet

Receiving attention from the vet is a fact of life for horses, and it is better for all concerned if veterinary visits can be as stress-free as possible. It is your job to ensure that your horse is prepared. If you have problems make sure you work on perfecting the respect, attention and leading lessons. If your horse dislikes having strangers in his stable then invite all your horsy friends round and get your horse accustomed to new people in his territory. Set the situation up so that he learns that any visit can be pleasurable.

We do know of one yard where the owner has unfortunately misunderstood the teaching of an enlightened horseman. The horses have not been taught to respect any human's space or wishes. Consequently every time something such as farriery or dental work needs to be done the vet has to sedate each horse. The owner cannot even turn the horses out with ease. This is not a happy situation for either owner or horses. Horses like to know their boundaries and expect leadership.

Box walking

This is when a horse spends the majority of his time in the stable walking round and round. It is traditionally thought to be caused by boredom or stress, although pain may also be a factor. If you have ever had a bad back you will know that you often reach a point where you need to walk around in order to relieve the pain. The same could apply to the horse. It is important to establish the reason for the behaviour and deal with the real cause. Other remedies, such as putting tyres or similar obstacles in the stable to hinder the horse's movement, only serve to add further hassle to his life.

Bucking

Horses may buck, simply out of the sheer joy of life, at any age. Just watch horses in a field; they often buck just for fun. It would be wrong to punish a horse for just being a horse.

But sometimes horses buck because they are in pain – possibly from an ill-fitting saddle or bridle, or because they have an injury (which the rider may not even be able to detect). As part of your horse's regular maintenance programme you should have his teeth attended to by an equine dental technician, check the fitting of his tack regularly and, if you are concerned about possible back problems, seek the advice of a vet or suitably qualified therapist.

Bucking may also develop because a horse works out that his rider has an insecure seat and so he can easily rid himself of the incumbrance. Regular riding lessons are a must for every horse owner. After all, a rider may be creating a problem, for example by hitting the horse in the sides with spurs because he or she does not have sufficient control of the lower legs. In such cases you would expect the horse to react in some manner.

A beautifully bred youngster was sent away to be started by a professional who was recommended in the locality. The horse was returned to the owners and the trainer advised turning the horse away for six months. The owners asked if everything was okay and were told yes, fine, but that the horse would now benefit from a rest.

After six months the owners brought the horse up, did some preliminary work and then tried to get on. The horse went crazy. The trainer was contacted and maintained that all had been well. Eventually, with help from other trainers, the horse was started.

Progress was not easy and in trying to get to the bottom of the problem the owners eventually discovered that the horse's withers had, at some point, been fractured. It transpired that this had occurred when he first went away to be backed. He had been difficult, had reared up and the trainer had pulled him over backwards. The damage and increasing pain from the injury meant that the horse had to be destroyed.

In Chapter 5 the importance of introducing the first saddle correctly was stressed. If this part of starting is carried out improperly the horse may have an issue with wearing a saddle and this often manifests in bucking performances. In such instances, the only real solution is to go right back to basics and convince the horse that the saddle (and eventually the rider) is not a big issue.

Cribbing and windsucking

These are so-called stable vices, although if these habits are really well established a horse will perform his tricks when living out in a field too. To crib, a horse takes hold of the stable door or any other handy object with his teeth and sucks in air. Windsuckers do not need to take hold of anything; they can just stand in the stable or field, arch their necks and gulp in air.

These habits often start as a reaction to stress, perhaps because the horse is confined to his stable for long periods, or because he is left for hours without sufficient fibre. If you catch your horse in the early stages of cribbing then change his management so that he has a more natural lifestyle. If in winter you have to stable him ensure he has plenty of hay or short-chop feeds to keep him occupied. Remember that the horse is designed to spend at least 16 hours out of every 24 eating. If he cannot do this he has to occupy his mouth in some other way!

The old-fashioned view is that such 'vices' will be copied by other horses stabled close by. However, research has shown that this is not necessarily the case. Your horse's management and his natural inclination will, however, have a bearing on whether the problem develops.

Difficult to bridle and saddle

The root of this problem usually lies in the starting process. If the bridling or saddling is rushed, or something goes wrong or the horse is not adequately prepared, problems will follow. They may be addressed immediately, or may be only partially resolved in which case they will resurface at some point in the future. For long-lasting results you need to go back to basics (see Chapter 5).

Other points to consider in such situations are poor-fitting tack and insensitive handling when tacking up. Horses only need one experience to learn something so they will remember if you bang the bit against their teeth and next time may not open their mouths so that you can insert the bit. Place the saddle on the horse's back carefully, remembering to have the stirrups run up and the girth folded out of the way. Stirrups or girths slapping against the sides of a sensitive horse are not appreciated!

Do girth up carefully as most horses blow themselves out when they feel the girth being buckled. If your horse hates being girthed and shows his feelings by trying to bite or kick, do check that he is not sore in that area (perhaps from chafing). If you watch your horse's breathing you can time the pulling up of the girth, with the in-breath, to cause least discomfort. Do up the girth gradually over a period of minutes and ensure that it is snug but not cripplingly tight.

Bridling problems can arise as the horse is particularly sensitive around his ears. You should make it your aim to be able to handle your horse everywhere – if this is done when the horse is young there is not

usually a problem. Older horses can learn to like being handled all over their bodies – grooming or massaging them usually provides an avenue which is enjoyable for them. If your horse is anxious about you touching a certain part of him then you can apply the approach-and-retreat method, gradually moving closer to his ear, or whichever area it is, rather than just making a grab for the sensitive spot.

Getting your horse used to being touched around his ears may take some time. In the interim period you may have to take the bridle to pieces in order to tack him up. Headshy horses are also difficult to bridle – hanging large strips of paper in their stable usually accustoms such horses to being touched on the head.

Difficult to clip

John Rarey, writing on horses in the 1800s, said: 'We can, in compliance with the laws of his nature, by which he examines all things new to him, take any object, however frightful, around, over, on him, that does not inflict pain – without causing him fear.' Here was a man who worked with horses on a daily basis and who clearly understood the responsibility we have to work out how a horse perceives the world before moving through each task in the training process.

As with every aspect of training horses, your first chance is your best chance. The first thing to do with a genuine youngster is work to get his respect and attention. This is so important. A horse has to know you're important to him and vice versa. He has to be listening before you can teach him anything. To help with this you should do a little in-hand work, like moving him a step towards you, backing him up, moving the quarters and so on. When a horse is responding softly without effort, his head will drop, he'll get a soft eye and he'll probably lick and chew. For your horse's sake please use a standard headcollar only. Training/pressure halters are never recommended because the result you get is never genuine but forced.

When a horse is soft and relaxed he'll be receptive for you to begin the lesson. Michael likes to have a 16½ft (5m) clip rope because it's easy to handle and at the same time you have enough rope to give your horse a bit of space if he needs it. He likes to work in an open space like a manège or small paddock for the

By the time I saw Michael at the *Your Horse* magazine reader day, I had spent two winters battling to get my horse clipped and had tried a variety of methods. As Michael worked on a horse with a shoeing problem he mentioned that he could also cure clipping problems and I suddenly started to pay a lot more attention. I bought Charlie, a 16.3hh Irish Draught cross hunter, in the summer as a six-year-old. His previous owner had only had him a short time; he had been taken in part exchange for a horsebox, and though she had intended to hunt him she decided he was too small! I assumed he had been clipped in the past, but she could not say for sure.

As Charlie and I got to know each other it became clear that he was not the bravest animal on four legs. There is one corner of the indoor school which still has him worried after two years, so I was not surprised to be dragged to the muck heap as soon as the clippers were turned on. I duly rang the vet and picked up some ACP tablets. I was advised to start with six tablets, although up to 18 would be safe for a horse of his size. After Charlie had had 15 tablets with no sign of drowsiness we twitched him and went for it. On this, the second attempt at clipping, we got some of his shoulder hair off before we were so battered and bruised that we decided to call it a day. Charlie was turned out into a small paddock, where he immediately began staggering about, the ACP taking effect now that his adrenaline levels were coming down.

At this point I would have called it a day, but Charlie was competing at local dressage shows and he sweated up so much during daily schooling sessions that I decided to keep going. However, I called in a friend, Angie, who works with flighty Thoroughbred eventers, and with the aid of the twitch we managed to tidy up his clip slightly; I had to part his mane down the middle and go without plaiting to cover up the bad bits! I spent night after night through that winter 'playing the clippers' to Charlie.

I also went to see a demonstration by a world-famous horse whisperer and during the break asked him about my clipping problem. He suggested starting with a hair dryer as it makes a similar noise and moves the hair but gives the horse a pleasant warm feeling. What a good idea I thought, so I spent the next few months blow-drying my horse! This worked fine; Charlie is now completely fine with a hair dryer, but it had no effect on his clipper phobia!

I began rugging Charlie in the following August in the hope that he wouldn't grow a coat, but by October it was clear that we were going to have to try again. Angie and I decided to give him one more go before resorting to getting him sedated, something I really did not want to do, especially after the ACP had had so little effect. I was afraid that Charlie would need dangerous levels of sedation to make it possible to clip. We twitched him and I held on while he virtually lay on the floor groaning through the whole thing. We managed a sort of trace clip, but I was left feeling guilty and vowing never to put my horse through that again.

I bought some cordless clippers, designed for Thoroughbreds, and spent another winter playing them to Charlie. This time, with no dangling wire, I was able to move around him in the stable and even conned him into letting me clip two small patches off each shoulder, which I proudly pointed out to anyone who would listen. But it was obvious that I was never going to be able to clip him properly and I was at the end of the line.

It was then I found myself at the *Your Horse* reader day watching Michael quietly working with a youngster who had been banned by most of the farriers in his area. I was particularly impressed with the fact that Michael did not use the 'send away' method of join up. This was because a man teaching 'natural horsemanship' had already tried that with Charlie, the result being that Charlie never 'joined up' and just raced round and round till he was dripping with sweat and eventually fell over. I truly believe that Charlie would have kept going till he had a heart attack and died.

So I booked onto one of Michael's weekend courses, hoping to learn about his methods and perhaps try to work on Charlie's clipping problem. After half an hour of Michael working with Charlie, I was in the round pen rubbing the clippers all over my horse, almost crying with relief that we had got to this point without causing any fear, pain or danger to Charlie. Charlie now sports a very smart full clip and is looking forward to being a lot less sweaty during schooling sessions!

same reason. Working in a stable can be a bit too restrictive for a horse; it may take the pressure off you, but the confinement often puts pressure on the horse. Horses are more comfortable in larger spaces, and if it is practical you should help them by moving outside or into a bigger stable to help them.

Rechargeable clippers will give you the freedom of movement necessary for this exercise. The battery in these usually lasts for at least one-and-a-half hours on the fast speed and three hours on the slow speed which is plenty of time to get a horse clipped. It is perfectly all right to use standard clippers with a flex because the principles are exactly the same, but cordless clippers are an excellent development and help to make the job much simpler.

Introducing the clippers for the first time

(see systematic desensitisation, pages 86–7) Feed out about 6½ft (2m) of rope to the horse so that he is well out of your space before turning the clippers on. A young horse who has never heard or seen them before will be curious about the vibrating noise. This curiosity is a good thing but very fragile, and it will take him through the lesson successfully as long as you preserve it. Don't over-expose him to the point that he becomes frightened. Give a horse space when you first turn the clippers on.

As you would expect, a horse will become a little tense at this point. You'll see in his expression that he wants to investigate but can't bring himself to. His head will be raised and there will be more activity in the ears and eyes. If you've given your horse enough space he shouldn't find it necessary to move away from you. You should keep the clippers running until his head drops and his pulse rate reduces. When this happens you can turn the clippers off. Each exposure like this will build a horse's tolerance to the clippers.

You should repeat this process again a few times before getting closer. It is essential to take the time to get this presented correctly now because it will set a horse up for life. From this point on, the success of this lesson depends on your ability to read your horse. Your aim is to preserve the horse's curiosity while decreasing the distance between you until you make contact with the clippers. Don't be in a hurry. Remember you are not clipping your horse today; you are schooling him to accept the clippers for the future. Remember that every step towards your goal is as

1 You'll find that young horses accept the clippers on the lower part of their neck much more readily than nearer the head. As you progress along the horse's body make sure you check on how she's dealing with things. You can see from her face that she's paying attention

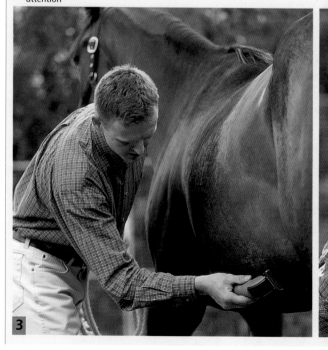

The correct approach to clipping

All young horses who go to Michael to be schooled for clipping have left with the perception that it is no more frightening than being groomed or rubbed all over. Many even enjoy the experience because of the vibrating/massaging effects of the clippers on their skin. This is how it should be. It is all to do with presentation: if presented well it's easy for a horse to accept, if done badly a horse will fear it. There is no reason why older horses with a phobia of clipping should not be successfully retrained.

2 Allow the horse to watch you all the way if that's what she wants to do. It makes it easier for her to see that the clippers are harmless

3 Once she's comfortable with you working the clippers up high progress to more vulnerable areas like under the belly, legs and head

4 Most horses are bound to be sceptical of having the clippers near their head, so take your time. The first presentation is the most important, so make sure that you get it right. Her raised head and

pricked ears here show that she finds this quite difficult, so keep your hand in this position to give her a few seconds to consider it

5 Be aware that the vibration of the clippers through the horse's head can cause her trouble. Look at her ears: one ear is considering a possible escape if it should become necessary, while the other ear is dealing with the clippers. The soft eye and the lowering of the head suggest that she's coping with it all quite well

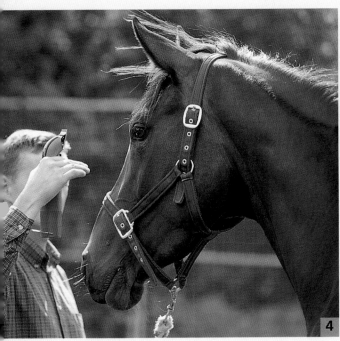

important as the first. A mistake at any time during the building process can take you right back to square one.

As you work to decrease the distance between horse and clippers your horse may feel the need to move away. Our natural reaction when this happens is to try and hold him still. This causes tension in a horse and he'll feel more reason to resist. You should direct him around you so that he is able to move, but so that you can maintain your position and continue to work with the clippers. This is not as easy as it sounds because if you move too slow a horse will realise that he can evade you by moving away. On the other hand, if you move too fast a horse will feel like you are chasing him with the clippers.

Common problems

- The presentation of the clippers can be too hasty. The horse becomes panicked and the clippers are turned off. From a horse's point of view, this behaviour paid off because it removed the thing he was afraid of. Technically the person has rewarded the wrong behaviour; the handler may have made contact with the clippers, but inadvertently caused the horse pain, and so made the horse suspicious of the clippers again.
- The horse will be hurt if the edge of the clipper blade spikes him; this can happen if the clippers are not held flat to his skin.
- The blade may become too hot if the clippers have not been adjusted correctly or have been running for an extended period of time.
- Blunt blades may cause the clippers to pull at the skin and nip.

All these can create a clipping phobia in a horse, and in most cases there is a genuine anxiety or even fear; being hard on a horse will not help. The ideal way to work is to ensure your presentation is progressive and so avoid problems occurring in the first place. In other words, slow everything down.

Difficult to groom

Grooming is usually a pleasurable experience for horses; they indulge in mutual grooming when at liberty so you may assume they would like to be groomed by humans too. However, if your horse

doesn't like it ask yourself whether you are being too heavy-handed on him, or maybe using such a light touch that you are irritating him. What he will appreciate are firm but loving touches, applied in a rhythmical manner. If he has a sensitive area, such as his belly, take care when touching him here. Get him used to the feel of your hand, or use a grooming glove made from soft, fleecy material. If he tries to bite or kick you when you make contact, ensure you are safe and keep your hand in position. Once he relaxes you can take your hand away. If you remove your hand when he threatens you, he is learning how to control your movements. If you ignore his threats and only remove your hand when he has relaxed, you are teaching him to accept your touch everywhere.

Difficult to rug up

Horses who do not like having their bodies touched may also dislike having rugs on. They may try to nip the handler or may kick out as leg straps or cross surcingles are fastened. Getting the horse accustomed to having items on him and having straps around the legs is essential. See Chapter 4 for a step-by-step guide to systematic desensitisation.

Jumping problems

These can manifest as a refusal to jump, running out, rushing or lack of impulsion. Jumping problems are often rooted in the rider. One way to establish whether this is the case or not is to loose jump the horse so that you can see how he goes. If he jumps happily but the problem reappears when he is ridden then it is up to the rider to be honest and recognise his or her faults. The good news is that rider problems can be addressed through good instruction. Even problems such as lack of confidence or fear can be resolved now, through the use of sports psychology techniques.

If a horse is unhappy when jumping loose then other factors need to be considered. These include:

- Is the horse physically, mentally and emotionally able to cope with what is being asked?
- Is there a problem with the surface on which he is jumping, for example is it slippery, or too deep?

Could this be causing a loss of confidence on the horse's part?

- Does the horse have an injury that is causing him pain?
- Is the horse genuinely frightened and, if so, why?

There is always a reason for a horse's behaviour – the difficult part is discovering the true cause. Sometimes this is rather like peeling the layers off an onion. You find what you think is the cause, only to discover that there's another layer or problem lurking underneath! However, if you keep on thinking and looking you will get to the root of the problem.

Leading

Being able to get your horse's respect and attention and lead him wherever you wish is an essential element for successful horse handling. If you can lead your horse well you often find that other problems do not happen. Many of the difficulties Michael deals with are actually resolved or eased once he has the horse leading properly.

See the guidelines on leading in Chapter 5. Investing effective time in this one area will reap tremendous benefits.

Loading

Before even considering loading a horse you must be able to get his attention, lead him and move him around as and when you want. It is sensible to have the trailer or lorry in an inviting situation, where the ramp is not too high and the ground around the trailer is not too slippery. You want the horse to make a conscious choice to go into the vehicle. Therefore the advice that is often given, to park the vehicle directly outside the stable, or alongside a wall so the horse cannot escape that way, is not very helpful. It only serves to cut down the horse's options and takes responsibility and choice away from him.

When loading your horse you do not want to enlist people to gang up on him. You want to set the situation up so that the horse finds it easy to do the right thing and load into the vehicle. Check that everything works towards the end goal – for instance,

side gates on a ramp may hinder you if it is possible to get the rope caught in them. If this happens when your horse is trying you out, you will be at a disadvantage and your horse may try to exploit this. The end result is you have a more difficult situation to deal with.

Probably the most difficult thing to do when loading is to allow the time it takes. Most people try to rush things and as a result interfere at the wrong moment, so putting the horse off the job in hand. Work second by second, watching how the horse reacts and rewarding the slightest try. Be aware of your body position as you do not want to block your horse. Ensure that you do your loading practice at home when you can spend the necessary time. It is a common fault for people not to bother until the day of the show – which is when everyone gets fraught.

If your horse gets stuck at the bottom of the ramp using the quarter rope may help, although it should not be used to pull the horse around. The rope is intended to get the horse moving his quarters again. Observe your horse carefully to check whether the quarter rope is causing him trouble or not. Some horses will fight more and so you can add to your problems.

If this happens the key is to get your horse to move from the harder position. You need to rediscover the softness within him that is essential for training. This may mean taking him away from the trailer or lorry and working to regain respect and attention somewhere else before returning to the loading.

AVOID WELL-WISHERS – AND KEEP CALM

If you are at a show and your horse will not load, then do not let other 'well-meaning' people 'help' by throwing water, lunge lines, brushes, whips and whatever else at the horse. Shouting, and misusing pressure halters, are also common practice and should be avoided. In most cases such 'help' only serves to make things worse in the long term.

A common nightmare: loading and unloading

This is the area where many people have problems. From the horse's point of view it is very unnatural to go willingly into a confined space which is often dark and smells strange. When they are bundled into a trailer or lorry and the whole thing moves, bumping along fields and swinging around corners, all at great speed with little consideration for the horse inside, it is hardly surprising that they do not relish loading and travelling.

If the horse also happens to be claustrophobic or has an accident when loading, travelling or unloading, this compounds the initial problem. Often people create difficulties for themselves and their horses because they give the horse a poor introduction to the process and then never allow enough time to school the horse to accept this aspect of life.

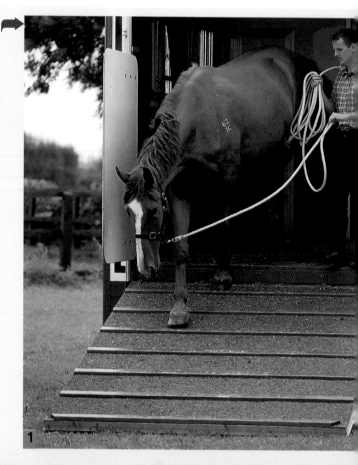

1

3

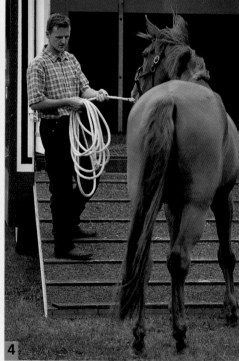

4

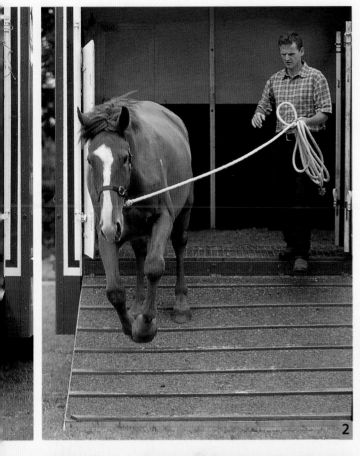

1–2 When a big horse decides he wants to get out of the lorry quickly let him do so. Feed him the rope and stay out of his way. Trying to slow him down will only make him move faster. Conversely, allowing him to do it at his own speed will take the pressure off him and he'll slow himself down

3–4 When a horse plants himself you have to do something to get his feet moving. Stepping to one side or the other and asking from your new position will lift a horse's shoulder into movement

5 When the decision is made a horse will often go all the way into the lorry in one go

6 Be sure to reward him: give him lots of praise and make him feel comfortable

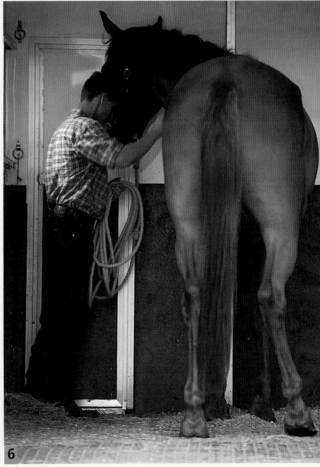

Your job is to set the situation up so that it is easy for the horse to do the right thing. If this is not happening you need to reassess what you are doing and change whatever it is that is not working.

Napping

Horses nap (ie refuse to go forwards) for many different reasons. Most commonly it's due to a fear of something unknown or something they associate with a previous bad experience. At other times it may simply be because they don't want to do what the rider is asking, perhaps because they would prefer to be back in their field or stable. Before we begin to deal with a napping problem we have to know what's going on in a horse's mind. If a horse is afraid we must help him out; if he's lazy, we must tell him to get on with it.

Most of the time horses nap because they are afraid, but unfortunately most riders assume they are being bad or lazy and get tougher on them. If you think of it from a horse's point of view this makes

things much worse. What they would really appreciate is some sympathy.

If you can genuinely share your horse's feelings you would sympathise. These days, humans rarely experience real fear and so it is difficult for us to understand exactly what it is like for a horse when he sees something he doesn't want to go past. Take a rubbish bin, for example. We, as humans, understand that these things are not dangerous, but from the horse's viewpoint there is something with which he is not familiar and which could threaten his life.

Just think of the men who have to lead soldiers into the many dangerous conflicts around the world. In these circumstances everyone will be afraid but shouting, bullying and threatening will not work. All it does is damage the people who have to be motivated to do their job. They need trust and support. It is not to say that they don't have to get their job done – they do – but they need help to achieve it.

There are situations where young horses feel this fear too and we have to be sympathetic to that. Instinct will be telling them not to go past something,

■ Napping: in this case it is the front of the horse that needs correcting. Michael will pick up his right hand to correct the horse to the direction of the movement he wants. His left leg supports this action. All aids should be used just to correct and not to confront a horse, and Michael is using neither his inside leg nor outside hand here

and yet often we're told to get tougher on them and make them get on with it. We have to understand that a lack of empathy will cause that horse to become less responsive to our lead, whereas an increase in empathy will encourage a horse to try a little harder for us in spite of its fears. This is what we want.

All we need to do is get a horse to try and he'll do the rest for us, whether it's jumping a bigger jump or conquering a fear. So how can you help your horse? The first thing to understand is prevention is better than cure. Ideally you want to build your horse's confidence over some weeks so that he doesn't get frightened by anything while out on a hack. Underlying everything is a trust that you must have developed through every part of the training process. Every second you handle him (even in the stable) he must know that if he can't handle something you're going to help him. This is most important. Secondly you can actively help him to develop his confidence by setting up little tasks for him in the controlled environment of his home.

Our job is to try to develop a horse's ability to stop,

think and look for a solution rather than run away at top speed. Setting up little tasks like walking through a river or over a scary piece of plastic will get a horse thinking this way. By giving him the time and encouragement he needs, you develop a horse's confidence. A horse will feel stronger having dealt with things that he previously would have run away from.

Think of how police horses are trained. The police do not expect a young green horse to go straight into a riot situation and cope with it. A mounted police officer wants his horse to be absolutely in control of his fears in any kind of situation, so the horses are well prepared at home. They face all kinds of tasks, each designed to develop the horse's confidence. Ordinary riders have to apply the same thought and training processes as none of us wants to find out that our

HELP YOUR HORSE WITH HIS PROBLEM

The idea of jumping off and leading your horse past an obstacle goes against what is normally taught. Riders are told that they must not let the horse get away with misbehaving and must ride him past, otherwise they have lost. The horse does not see the situation in this light at all. If you get off a worried horse and lead him past the 'monster' he will regard you as helping him with this problem. He will not see your action as a weakness. You will have acted like a leader, and this is what you want because it builds trust.

horse is afraid of drain covers when we've got a queue of traffic passing us. In these circumstances you don't have the time you need to help your horse because of the added pressure from the motorists. The rider should jump off the horse and lead him past whatever is troubling him. When the pair gets home the rider should do some more preparation work with the horse. Ideally, you would prepare your horse first so that you don't get into this kind of situation.

If you follow the traditional advice that tells you to be tougher on your horse in this sort of situation, or if you put a stronger rider on to make him go past, you will exacerbate the problem. If a horse is worried the last thing he needs is a stronger rider. Think of this in simple horse terms. Let's say he gets a mile from home along the road and comes to a road sign that he doesn't like. A strong rider will be able to make him go past and will assume that everything is all right. The next day the horse remembers that this place was frightening for him so he tells you about it again. You ride him stronger and manage to get him past it. Again you think it's okay.

At this point, one of two things will happen. He may simply work out that this road sign is not frightening after all and with a bit of luck won't resent you too much for getting too tough on him. However, more commonly he'll recognise this place as

■ Helping a horse to find a way of dealing with something he finds fearful builds up the bond between horse and rider, and increases the horse's confidence in himself

somewhere where he gets frightened and will work harder at not going past it. On day three he will begin to object before he is even close to the road sign. In other words his napping will start closer and closer to home because of the anticipation of trouble ahead. The horse becomes worse and worse at hacking out. In extreme cases a horse may refuse to leave the yard because of this anticipation of trouble. Although it is rare, a horse may even be too afraid to leave his stable.

As riders we have to be careful that we do not embark on this slippery slope. We must not be too hard, but we must not be too easy either. It is all a question of balance. Consider young racehorses; they begin their careers with lots of enthusiasm, which keeps them going throughout a race with maximum effort. At the end of a race there is one common factor throughout the whole world: the winning line (or in fact the last 100m before the winning line, which has the grandstand with the public roaring, and which is also where jockeys ride at their strongest with whips, hands and heels). A young horse will run naïvely with maximum effort for the first few races of his life, but then mysteriously will seem to drop out in the last part of a race. This is often seen as a horse being ungenuine. Michael believes that a horse has simply become wise and sees the last 100m of a race as somewhere to avoid; he quite understandably doesn't want to get there.

You can apply this principle to many different disciplines, whether your horse is napping at the show ring, out on a hack, or at jumps. The key is to understand that he is probably genuinely frightened and needs you to help him out.

Picking up feet

Even horses in their teens can still have an issue with letting humans handle their feet. From the horse's viewpoint it is easy to understand why, but what is difficult to comprehend is how their owners have managed for so many years. Picking out of feet is a once, if not twice daily task, so it makes sense for your horse to be relaxed about the procedure.

Whether your horse is young or old, the principle behind teaching him to lift his feet and allow them to be held remains the same. See Chapter 5 for a step-by-step guide.

Rearing

If there is one equine activity which most riders really dislike it is rearing. Riders are in such a vulnerable position, especially as many lack the truly independent seat which allows them to stay in balance with a rearing horse. What often happens is that the rider hangs on via the reins. This can lead to the very dangerous situation of the horse falling over backwards, and as a result either the horse or rider, or both, can be injured.

Over the years countless pieces of advice have been handed out to those whose horses rear. These include such improbable remedies as 'smash an egg on the horse's head while he's in the air'. No one bothers to comment that this inevitably means that you have to carry a supply of eggs with you at all times! Other suggestions have included hitting the horse with a whip between the ears while he's in the air, or pulling him over and sitting on his head. Apart from taking a great deal of skill and balance, these things are rarely, if ever, effective, and not to be recommended.

There is a valid reason for everything a horse does and if he is doing something that we don't want him to do we have to take away his reason for doing it. Ridden horses will rear for many different reasons and it's our job to identify the cause and deal with it so that this adverse behaviour doesn't recur.

By the time a horse uses rearing as an objection he has usually become really quite negative. If a ridden horse finds something stressful, he will object quite subtly at first to give you the benefit of the doubt. He may shake his head or bore down with his head to release the reins if he can. If the rider doesn't help him he may try a little warning buck to show his disapproval. Over a period of time he may try to develop his buck until he can unbalance the rider, even if only for a split second. If he manages this he will keep working at it until a rider falls off.

If the rider is strong enough not to fall off and boots him through it, a horse will probably give up for a while, but only until he can think of something else to say in his quest to be heard. You may see a horse double things up and perhaps shake his head and buck at the same time. If he's still not listened to by the rider, he may gradually decide to stop moving forwards to the point where he refuses to go

1

2

← **A serious rearer**

This horse had been saying to previous riders that he had a problem, but they failed to understand his signals and told him off. What started out as a relatively small difficulty has now mushroomed into a big issue.

1 This horse reared as soon as Michael got on him – from the horse's point of view it was essential that he made his views clear first! This attitude has developed because the horse's earlier, subtler signs were not read correctly. He has therefore had to become more 'vocal' in order for people to listen to him. Unlike other riders, who have told the horse off for rearing, Michael does nothing other than ask the horse to go forwards on a loose rein. This different approach works because it is non-confrontational. The horse realises that this rider is listening to what he has to say

2 Only when the horse is relaxed does Michael ask for a trot. He appreciates every little effort made by the horse and lets the horse know that he is pleased with him

3 A few minutes later and they are happily cantering around. A simple shift of thinking and approach has ensured that this horse has enjoyed being ridden on this occasion. This can be built upon, but the regular rider needs to search in her memory so that the real reason for the rearing can be determined and resolved

3

forwards altogether. He may even spin around to the left or right to avoid the direction of work. A strong rider may be quick enough to keep him going, but all the time the resentment is growing and he'll be thinking of more and more to say. With his bucking option, his standing still option and his spinning round option shut down, a horse may try to run backwards but again a strong rider may beat him forwards and shut down this possibility too.

He now has only two options left: to go up in the air or to throw himself on the ground. By rearing up he usually finds the weakness he is looking for in a rider. It is rare these days to find a horse who has been so brutalised that he has to throw himself on the ground, but it does occur sometimes.

What started as a simple objection has escalated into quite an issue for both horse and rider. Our job as trainers is to pitch the horse's lesson correctly in the first place so that these objections don't arise. If we misjudge it and such behaviour does develop we must know how to smooth things over so that it doesn't get worse. It's the little things that make the difference; you must get help before things get too far out of hand.

The horse pictured was quite a way down the line and didn't even give Michael the chance to ask him to go forwards. He had got to the point where just having a rider on his back was enough to set him off into rearing. Michael was on him maybe five seconds before it began. His approach was to show the horse that he was not going to be forced forwards. He had to understand that Michael was on his side; he did not have to shout because Michael was listening to every little thing he said. In other words, the rider appreciated every little try, and if he was troubled by something, the rider helped him out with it.

A horse will spot this attitude in a rider within seconds. That's all this horse was ever trying to do in the first place – find someone to sympathise and help him through his day. But however loud he shouted he had not been heard. Many people can't see what a horse is thinking and assume he is just being bad when he doesn't want to do something. Consequently they get tougher on the horse and do more, when they should be doing less.

My first big demonstration in Denmark attracted 1,500 people and was held at an élite equestrian centre in the north of the country. Afterwards there was a lot of interest and many people came to talk to me and ask for advice. The crowd eventually dispersed and I picked up my kit bag and made my way out of the building to get something to eat.

A man and his young daughter who had also been at the demonstration approached me to ask if we could talk. The man told me that his daughter was very interested in my approach to horses. She said it was amazing and that she would desperately like to come and work with me in England if it was at all possible. At that time we were travelling quite a lot and it was difficult for me to plan for her to come and spend a block of time with me. I said that I would be around for the next few days and if she wanted to she could watch me working. Her name was Bianca and whenever I had a horse to work with, she always came to watch. At the time she was only 13 years old and didn't speak much English so she'd keep her distance and just watch to see what she could learn.

Bianca always wanted her own horse, but at that time she had to make do with a loan horse from the centre. The deal was that she would help out around the yard and would get to ride this horse – Sorte, a small Danish warmblood mare of about nine years old – in return as long as she wasn't needed for lessons. Bianca was able to ride Sorte because nobody else liked her. Sorte was a horse with a reputation for bucking everyone off when she'd had enough of them. Bianca liked her and treated her like her own and was never bucked off.

I could see how dedicated she was. She watched every second that she could and one day I told her to tack Sorte up and I'd give her a lesson. Sorte was a typical riding-school horse with dead sides, hard mouth and rigid outline. My thoughts were that this was going to be a difficult task in such a short time: a young girl who didn't speak much English, and a horse who wasn't really interested in changing very much.

Anyway, we set to work. I showed Bianca how to get Sorte swinging along by opening the left and right rein alternately and cueing the hind legs at the most opportune time to get them off the ground. Instantly there was a magnificent change. Both horse and rider looked so much freer and now we had something to work with... we had the forward movement and softness which is the basis of everything.

Bianca had the biggest smile you've ever seen on her face. It was such a simple technique but it had a huge impact on her horse. It was so different to everything she'd ever been taught by her instructor. I explained that her poor little horse had never known how to move before because the riders she had were being taught to sit so still and rigid. I told her to go away and practise this swing and see how big and loose she could get the walk and trot.

It was going to be difficult because sometimes Bianca would only be allowed to ride her horse once or twice each week, and at other times Sorte would be ridden in a lesson taught by a conventional instructor at the centre. In spite of this, Bianca worked undeterred and continued to improve the horse's way of going. On top of that, whenever she rode the instructors would frown upon her because of her loose reins and swinging legs. Bianca knew that for now this was what Sorte needed. It made Sorte happy and this young girl had the courage of her convictions to stick with it.

Whenever I returned to Denmark I would always give Bianca a lesson and plenty of homework to go on with while I wasn't around. Very soon she was able to ask her horse to flex at the poll and collect up without any force. Bianca transformed Sorte, who as a result turned into one of the nicest rides at the centre.

It wasn't long before everyone saw the difference Bianca had made in Sorte, but the downside was that suddenly everyone wanted to ride the mare. Obviously Bianca wasn't very keen on this but could do nothing because Sorte wasn't her horse. Unfortunately, the opportunity for Bianca to ride became less and less because everyone else was riding Sorte, and some weeks she wouldn't be allowed to ride her at all. She was only able to help Sorte if she could ride her but this was out of her control.

I wanted to include this story because it shows how important it is to be genuine and dedicated. Bianca has both these qualities, and her motivation was simply to help her little horse have a better life even if it was against all the odds. What I learned from this is that there is only so much you can do, but that you should still do it to the best of your ability if there's a chance it will do some good. I must admit I would have found it difficult to continue work on a horse knowing that my work was going to be undone over the next few days.

The fact is that Bianca did make a difference to this horse's life in spite of the odds, and the work that they did together will have had a lasting and beneficial effect on the mare.

CASE HISTORY

CHECKLIST Take a moment to reassess what you have read so far.

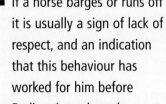

- If a horse barges or runs off it is usually a sign of lack of respect, and an indication that this behaviour has worked for him before
- Redirecting a horse's negative thought or action to a more positive action helps to show the horse that there is more benefit in positive behaviour
- A horse only needs one experience to learn something new
- If you present a new experience to a horse badly the chances are he'll fear it
- If your horse is not doing what you ask you should reassess what you are doing and change what is not working
- Napping can be caused by a number of factors: a fear of the unknown; a lack of confidence; and an association with a previous bad experience
- If a horse is doing something we do not like we have to take away his reason for doing it
- Horses are often labelled as problem animals through no fault of their own – usually because they have been handled by inexperienced people who have simply over-horsed themselves
- Horses like to know what the boundaries are in terms of acceptable behaviour
- It is wrong to punish a horse for acting like a horse
- There is always a reason for a horse's behaviour – the difficult part lies in discovering the true cause
- Work with your horse second by second, watch his reactions and reward the slightest try
- Your horse needs to know that if he cannot cope with something then you will help him out
- This attitude in your horse is built up through you showing him that he can trust you at all times

Conclusion

Having their own horse is the culmination of a dream for many people. If you are one of those who has experienced problems with your horse, if you thought that your dream was starting to turn sour, we hope that this book has shown you that anything is possible when you learn to think like a horse. It is true that if something is worth having it usually involves effort. Thinking like a horse is just the same; it is a skill that takes time to develop and refine. Now that you have the principles of Think Equus you can spend the rest of your life on a fascinating journey. This will apply whether you are working with a single horse and developing the communication to an amazing level, or dealing with many horses.

The joy of Think Equus is that you can apply the principles to horses all over the world and they will understand you. No matter what breed or sex or size, whether the horse is young or old, he will be able to relate to you. In their careers all horse people come across animals that are different to the norm – these are the problem horses which are maybe dealing with life by being angry and aggressive, or shut down and cold. In our fast-moving world where so much seems disposable, it is inevitable that horses will get a raw deal because some people cannot be bothered to meet their responsibilities.

To be a true horseman or woman you have to recognise not only your own responsibilities, but also those of your horse, and those you share. True horse people co-operate with horses so that each equal partner in the relationship receives benefit from the arrangement. The end result is that life is much more enjoyable for both. Each is able to learn in an atmosphere of trust and patience. Horses and humans feel safe, comfortable, respected, confident and loved, and are ready to face whatever life puts before them.

Useful Information

Michael Peace

If you would like to find out more about Think Equus, Michael Peace offers private lessons and consultations and runs a number of courses at his Oxfordshire base. The courses cover foundation work, effective riding, problems and starting the young horse. Participants attend with their horses and groups are kept small so that everyone gets individual attention. Students without horses can also be catered for. It is also possible to send horses to Michael for schooling. Lecture demonstrations are also held throughout Britain and abroad.

Contact Michael at PO Box 230, Kidlington, Oxfordshire, OX5 2TU. Tel/fax 01865 842806. Email: michael@thinkequus.com
Website:www.thinkequus.com

Lesley Bayley

Equestrian consultant and specialist Lesley Bayley offers freelance instruction in both riding and horse care. She takes a holistic approach to horse and rider, using both traditional and alternative methods, tailored to suit the needs of the individual. Lesley is based in Northamptonshire.

Contact her on 07774 226204. Email: lesley.bayley@virgin.net

Think Equus services

Private consultations
One of the most popular ways to get help for yourself and your horse is a private consultation. Michael will come to visit you wherever you are and work on whatever area of your horsemanship you wish to improve. Perhaps you need some direction with a young horse; have trouble with loading, shoeing, clipping, and leading or a riding/schooling problem. Whatever it is, these private visits are a very effective way to help you get the most enjoyment from your horse.

Send your horse for schooling
Whether you want your horse started correctly, ridden for the first time, made easier to handle, better to load, easier to clip, better to shoe or his/her ridden work improved, you can send your horse for a week or two with the guarantee that Michael will improve him or her beyond recognition.

Group tuition
If you have a group of friends who you think would like to know more about the Think Equus methods and philosophy we can arrange a half day or even a full day's education specifically tailored to your group's needs. Group tuition is excellent for riding clubs, college students, pony clubs or small private stables, and is recommended for groups of eight or less.

Clinic days
If you are a livery yard owner, manager of a riding school, or have access to suitable facilities, you may consider hosting a Think Equus clinic day. These are designed to encourage people in your local area to bring their horses on the day that Michael is visiting.

Think Equus courses and workshops
There are a number of Think Equus courses run by Michael Peace and his Think Equus team:

1 Two-day foundation course
   This two-day course is designed to give you the tools you need to build an effective partnership between you and your horse. It shows the importance of mutual respect and attention and covers the Think Equus method, basic equine behaviour and psychology. Michael recommends this course to anyone interested in horses at whatever level.
2 Ten-day starting the young horse course
   This is a ten-day course designed for those of you who want to be there to help your horse with his/her first saddle, bridle and rider. Participants are taught to use the Think Equus methods and encouraged to be as actively involved in the whole

process as possible. The course covers basic equine behaviour and psychology, join-up, long-lining and riding.

3 Five-day problem horse course

This course is the ideal situation for Michael to assess your working partnership with your horse and identify the things you need to change to get your horse working with you again. Over the five days of the course you will gain a unique insight into the psychology behind many of the common problems faced by horses and their owners. The course covers many of the Think Equus methods including join-up, long-lining and much more.

4 Five-day effective riding course

Whatever level your horse is at now, you will both benefit from the techniques learned in this course. The unique Think Equus riding techniques make it easy for your horse to give 100 per cent so you can both become the best you can possibly be.

All these courses require that you and your horse stay at Michael's stables in the beautiful Oxfordshire countryside. You will meet the Think Equus team and five other course members who will also share their experiences with you. For an application form please call Susi Peace on 01865 842806.

Demonstrations

If you have the drive and the determination, you may consider setting up a Think Equus public demonstration in your area. These demonstrations last on average for three hours and can attract hundreds of people. Your role will be to arrange a suitable venue, advertise in your local area, sell tickets and co-ordinate the event, as well as liaise closely with the Think Equus office. This option can be very good for attracting people to your centre and helping your business. However it is not for the weak-hearted and will take a lot of time and commitment from you. You will receive a percentage of each ticket sold.

Agents

We are looking for agents for the UK. If you are interested in arranging any of the above Think Equus services for friends or clients in your area please contact Susi Peace at our office.

Acknowledgements

I'd like to say thanks to my mum and dad for their selfless support, direction and encouragement in the early days of my career with horses.

Also my wife Susi for her love and enthusiasm over the past four years and without whom this book and many of our other projects would never have happened.

Many thanks to Lesley Bayley for her contribution and guidance through the trauma of my first book.

Finally but not least I'd like to dedicate this book to my one year old son Charlie for giving me a clearer perspective on life.

MICHAEL PEACE

I'd like to dedicate this book to my Mum, Dad and husband Martin for all their love, help and support over the years.

Very many thanks to Michael and Susi Peace – working with you both has been fascinating, and a real pleasure.

Finally, a special mention for a very special horse: Pride, who came into my life about ten years ago. She was the first mare I owned, is chestnut and is the most genuine, honest, kind horse anyone could ever wish to meet. If I have as much fun with her two sons as I have had with her I shall be well and truly blessed.

LESLEY BAYLEY

Index